A Flourishing Mind

Who are you *not* to flourish?

Suzanne Waldron

GOWOR
INTERNATIONAL PUBLISHING

A Flourishing Mind: Who are you *not* to flourish? © Suzanne Waldron 2014

www.suzannewaldron.com

The moral rights of Suzanne Waldron to be identified as the author of this work have been asserted in accordance with the Copyright Act 1968.

First published in Australia 2014 by Gowor International Publishing

www.goworinternationalpublishing.com

ISBN 978-0-9924977-9-8

Any opinions expressed in this work are exclusively those of the author and are not necessarily the views held or endorsed by Gowor International Publishing.

All rights reserved. No part of this publication may be reproduced or transmitted by any means, electronic, photocopying or otherwise, without prior written permission of the author.

Disclaimer

All the information, techniques, skills and concepts contained within this publication are of the nature of general comment only, and are not in any way recommended as individual advice. The intent is to offer a variety of information to provide a wider range of choices now and in the future, recognising that we all have widely diverse circumstances and viewpoints. Should any reader choose to make use of the information herein, this is their decision, and the author and publisher/s do not assume any responsibilities whatsoever under any conditions or circumstances. The author does not take responsibility for the business, financial, personal or other success, results or fulfilment upon the reader's decision to use this information. It is recommended that the reader obtain their own independent advice.

Dedicated to...

My mother-in-law Rosalie
My friend and mentor Fran
My surrogate family members Suzanne, Carol, and Robyn

My exceptional husband Phil, whom
I love and always will.
Thank you for being you and for
supporting me in being who I am.

A Personal Note From The Publisher

To the reader,

As the Founder of Gowor International Publishing, I make it part of my practice to offer a personal review of each of my authors' books. The reason I do this is so that you, the reader, can glean a further understanding of why this book is so valuable to you in your life.

The spirit within Suzanne is extraordinary. It's not very often that I come across people who are *truly* alive from a place very deep inside – and Suzanne is one of these. Ever since I first connected with Suzanne a year before this book was published, she has infused her enthusiasm and spark into my life. And what I love just as much as her dynamic presence and intoxicating charisma is just how deeply she bares her soul in the pages of this book.

I was moved to tears more than once reading *A Flourishing Mind*, and I was humbled, in awe of Suzanne's willingness to share the good, the bad, and the ugly with *you*, the reader – all so that you, too, may flourish. You will discover parts of yourself as you take a journey through Suzanne's life. You will liberate yourself from fear. You will feel that no matter what has happened to you, you can put one foot in front of the other and keep moving forwards.

Suzanne believes in your capacity to overcome the darkness and step into the light more than you may comprehend. But by the time you turn the last page of this book, it will be reverberating through every cell in your body. This is Suzanne's gift to you, and it's my every wish for you to receive it.

Enjoy the book.

With inspiration,

Emily Gowor
Founder of Gowor International Publishing

Contents

Foreword 3
Introduction 5
Chapter 1: Poison or Purpose? 13
Chapter 2: In Kind 33
Chapter 3: Beyond You 51
Chapter 4: Rampage Returns 73
Chapter 5: The Wonderful World of Aus 91
Chapter 6: To Evolve or Revolve? 113
Chapter 7: Alive & Kicking 131
Chapter 8: The Beauty in Death 153
Chapter 9: One Life Stand 167
Acknowledgments 177
Working with Suzanne 183
About The Author 188

Foreword

I find that today, more than ever before, people are longing for something more. People seem to want something more out of the time they spend at work, something more out of the time they spend with family, something more from their leisure time, and something more than they've ever had before.

If, as you read the passage above, you find yourself saying, 'No, that is not true for me. I am completely content. I am happy with myself just as I am now. I am fulfilled in all that I do, and in all of my relationships. I am satisfied with exactly what I have now and I do not long for more in any respect', then I suspect you are among a very special group of people.

In my thirty years in the people development industry and my thirty years in my own personal development journey, it is my experience that most people have a continued sense of longing. It is also my experience that there is a division between those people who achieve what they want to achieve in their adventures toward attaining that 'something more' and those who have an experience of escalating discontent and dissatisfaction as they fail to obtain that elusive 'something more'. I have spent the better part of thirty years wanting more myself, and also exploring the 'how'. I've read thousands of books, attended dozens of seminars, watched countless videos, and tried hundreds of methods in my own personal journey of growth, attainment, and achievement. I am fortunate to have experienced a great deal of the 'something more' and I've had some amazing mentors along the way.

Of all the books I've ever read about personal development journeys, *A Flourishing Mind* is one of the most compelling and transformational. My experience of this book was an awesome ride on the emotional roller coaster! I laughed, I cried, I felt anger and hurt, and I was lifted to great heights of joy, wonderment, and an abiding feeling of hope for the future. In this autobiography, Suzanne exposes her life in an open, honest, and direct way that had me captivated and frequently nodding in agreement saying 'Yes! Me too!'

I believe this book can and will reach the hearts and minds of all those who are fortunate enough to read it. It has answers to the 'how'. How do we survive the challenges that life presents? How do we continue to dream when dreams have been shattered? How do we pick ourselves up and keep going? How do we continue to grow and truly experience the real meaning of what it is to flourish? The stories and adventures shared in *A Flourishing Mind* culminate in messages of inspiration, hope, opportunity, abundance, joy, love, forgiveness and freedom.

Do read this book. Do give it to those you care for. Do share Suzanne's inspirational messages and guiding lights with everyone you know. In reading this book, I have been touched deeply, I have learned more about myself, I have grown and expanded my thinking, I am changed, and I am grateful.

Fran Berry
Director - Alive & Kicking Solutions

Introduction

Truly, this book has been written for you.

I believe I can do anything. I wasn't born that way; I learned to think that way. I also believe that because you were born in the same way (a clean slate, a few basic instincts, and some genetics in tow) that you also can do anything. This may sound strange, and you may want to quite rightly question my belief. I have learned over recent years that we have control over our innermost feelings and thoughts, and the more we are consciously aware, the more we can actively change anything we want. It's all a state of mind, and I've learned this. The amazing news is that because I've learned this, it means that you can learn it too.

This book is incredibly personal. There are no holds barred, no secrets, and no half-truths. I am laying myself bare to you. I choose to do this because what I have to say can be life changing, and I certainly changed my life for the better now that I know what I know. Seeing this story through my eyes will, I hope, open you up to a world of possibility, of what can be achieved in life.

Whilst reading this book you will discover more about yourself. While I recognise that a great deal of this story is mine, I guarantee you will find yourself in here somewhere. Even though you may not have experienced exactly the same events in life as me, I am certain you will identify with the raw emotions and feelings of hard times, both personally and professionally. I decided to write this story because I now have a beautiful life despite living through adversity, terror and hardship. I have undoubtedly worked hard for this. I believe in myself now more than ever, and if allowing you to experience my story through the pages of this book creates even one moment of change for you, or if it enhances your existence in even the smallest of ways, I feel that my mission in life is complete.

What I intend is for you to experience a mindset shift, a physical change, any sort of movement if you are stuck or feeling average – yes, I have high expectations! I believe you will be completely connected to this story when you read about how heart-wrenching life can be, as I am sure you too have had hard times. I am also certain that when you read about the kindness that comes with such heart-wrenching experiences, you will feel as I do: grateful to be included in humanity.

This book has been written to uplift you and inspire you to reach all that you are meant for, in whatever context: life, work, relationships or spirituality. Whether you are a leader, a businessperson, a parent, a family member, or a friend, I already know what you are capable of, and this book will support you in uncovering more of what you already know about yourself and expand your belief in yourself so much that when you're at the end of the book you will be raring to do, be, and act to achieve all that you desire. You are incredible, and anything you want to have, achieve, think or feel is possible.

Forgive me ahead of time, as I tend to get to the heart and core of deep and meaningful conversations very quickly. I don't generally take part in small talk! If you're a bit wary that perhaps I'm wearing rose-coloured glasses or I'm a fluffy 'rah rah' idealist and you don't believe that you are indeed this incredible, keep on reading and let me know on which page you finally realise you are capable and worthwhile – seriously, email me (my contact details are at the end of the book). If you already know what's possible and that you as a human being have all the potential in the world, then I welcome you to enjoy the story and reap the rewards of thinking in a way that expands and grows your life and to join me and the other readers in continuing to fuel the world with self-belief, kindness, and choice in life.

This is written solely from my perspective, my learning, and my memory. I am deeply appreciative of all the people who contributed to the difficult times in my life – as without them I wouldn't be as strong and resilient as I am today and in the fortunate position to share my learning with the world. I love, forgive, and cherish every moment of my life. I am equally grateful to those who have shown me the lighter side of life and given of themselves selflessly to help me overcome internal mental and external environmental challenges. I continue to learn from them, and it never ceases to amaze me how the right people come into our lives at the right time, giving us the right message.

The trick is to be open to those messages and to see beyond ourselves. First, we need to get a clear view, and that's what this book will help you achieve.

I was recently lying in bed, simply reflecting on my day, and as I lay there I suddenly got excited and a deep inner sense of loving myself occurred and I shouted out to my husband, 'I love who I am, I bloody love my life!' What a moment to behold! This is the whole reason behind the book, as I want more and more people to feel great about themselves and their accomplishments (both externally with material things and internally with feelings and emotions, self-esteem and confidence). The reason I chose the title *A Flourishing Mind* is that human flourishing is so incredibly wonderful to watch and experience. I absolutely believe I have flourished and continue to flourish. In fact, when I was thinking of the title for this book, the word 'flourish' popped up, completely unprompted, in so many conversations about me with other people. Isn't it awesome when the world is telling you something?

As you read this book I ask you to hold yourself, take care of yourself, allow yourself to feel and be absorbed but not to be carried away by the sadness or negative emotions the story may trigger. It's important that you focus on the parts that show hope and determination – the sadder parts of the story are simply there to include fact and provide depth to the reality of what I personally experienced. I hope the story is received with the intention of assisting and supporting generative thinking and giving hope to those who need it, and that it is enjoyed along the way. Take what you need, disregard the rest, and generate your own momentum in such a way that you will never leave this world with a doubt or regret.

'This is the great joy of life: to be used for a purpose recognized by yourself as a great one; to be a force of nature and not some sniveling clod of ailments and grievances complaining that the world will not devote itself to making you happy. I believe that my life belongs to the whole community and while I live it, I will give it as much as I can. I intend to be thoroughly used up when I die because I find the harder I work the better I live. For me life is no brief candle but some sort of splendid torch that I've got hold of for the moment and I intend to make it burn as brightly as I can before passing it on the next generation.'

George Bernard Shaw

'If you're going through hell, keep going.'

Winston Churchill

Chapter 1
Poison or Purpose?

'Mummy, Daddy was with a lady in bed this morning.'

These are some of the most damaging words I remember uttering as a small child. It seems this was the turning point in my life, this revelation to my mother. Before this, the world seemed so normal, so everyday and average. As you and I know, the world and everything in it can change in an instant.

I specifically remember seeing my father that day naked with another female in my parents' bedroom. It was early in the morning, and I had risen from my sleep, looking for someone to help me get dressed for the day. Rubbing my eyes and standing on the cold landing in front of my parents' bedroom in my nightie, I looked into the bedroom to see my father in all his pale white skin, his big belly and broad shoulders scurrying towards me, shooing me away from the room. His mistress was covering herself with the light-green bed covers, wide-eyed and shocked at my presence, slightly shying away from my view.

As a child, this discovery, albeit unusual in itself, wouldn't usually carry any deep significance or conscious meaning in the moment. Taking the experience very literally, I simply repeated my observation to my mother later that day. Of course, as we all know, being adults, this was a big deal, especially since this 'lady' was a teenager still at school and my father was in his mid-forties. From memory, I was between the ages of six and eight at the time. Suddenly my life veered off in a new, completely different direction. My world turned from feeling secure and safe to unpredictable, emotional, damaging and confusing. Once the secret had been revealed, there were angry faces in our house. There was a tense, growing sense of conflict, a feeling of blackness. Confrontations between my parents were frequent, increasing the shouting and crying which eventually led to their marriage falling apart.

Born in the late seventies into a small family in the United Kingdom, the first five years of my life were somewhat ordinary, with two working parents. We lived in a small council home in the countryside near a main town in Kent. We had a horse, friends and I had a sense as a small child of what I can describe as an inner feeling of security and love, perhaps unusually; both my parents were international truck drivers who drove and delivered all sorts of goods around Europe. You'd be surprised at how many different objects there are in the back of those trucks you see moving from one place to another. As part of their working lives, my parents delivered warm, juicy oranges to Spain, hardwired radio parts to Germany, and even Princess Diana's ski clothes to London! Working hard, they were doing well in their business and in the prime of their lives living a working person's existence – until my revelation, that is.

Naturally, many of my early memories include my father. He was born in the southeast of London into a poor life in the 1940s. As a rough and tumble man, he thought beating someone to a pulp in an argument was winning the point and therefore something to be proud of, as winning was his endgame. He was a dangerous man in this way – very tough and reckless with his anger. In the nature of polarity, he flirted, played, and enticed people with his danger, especially girls. Having already been married once before my mother, his life seemed at that point to allow him to get away with anything by simply bullying his way through situations using a confusing mix of intimidation and charisma. This danger was something I felt early on in my life, although my father was my hero and I was certainly Daddy's girl. I loved him; I sometimes feared him too.

He had an ability to lure you into a false sense of security with his wit and charm, though that could change at any minute and he was unpredictable. I certainly knew he would do anything for me, his little girl. It's hard to talk about, as I've always had a loving respect for him and his moments of support, loyalty and kindness. The good in him existed; I saw it, felt it. Though there was an exactly opposite side that scared me and shaped me through my younger years.

My mother was one of very few female truck drivers in Europe, and being a five-foot tiny thing with a big mouth and strong, toned muscles, she was simply a lean, mean driving machine! It's safe to say that she was, and is, a tomboy. She could certainly look after herself physically. It's harder to describe my mother in those early years. Any maternal connection was suppressed, if it was even there at all. Born into a family with four sisters, her own mother was killed in an accident when she was eight years old. Her father, as a single man, brought the children up in the 1960s whilst working and building his own fortune as an oil tanker driver.

I remember the feeling of my life changing from calm to chaos in that moment, the moment of the revelation I shared with my mother that her husband was in bed with another. Shortly after, my father moved out of our family home and into my grandmother's little old two-bedroom home. Surprisingly, he took his new girlfriend with him and they embarked on a new life together with both determination and the somewhat expected ridicule from the community of friends who remained in our lives. It has always amazed me, even as an adult, that my grandmother took them both in, knowing the seriousness of his actions. She literally gave up her bed and moved into the spare room of her own house whilst her shamed son continued on with his taboo affair. I wonder how other mothers would react? That said, on some level it doesn't surprise me at all, as my Grandmother was a beautiful, giving soul who supported and believed in her family and her only son. Her actions showed empathy, and her understanding showed strength of character.

Whilst my father and his girlfriend settled in together, I remained with my mother in our family home. My mother, being an international truck driver, took me with her when she wanted or was able to, and at other times, I've since learned, would leave me at a neighbour's house for days at a time without warning and without knowing how long she'd be gone. Perhaps she was finding life difficult, perhaps she couldn't cope; I don't know the reasons my mother put me into foster care. My life, which was already in pieces, was being further ripped apart by the fact that I was being sent away from home, away from my parents and the life and physical environment I knew so well. Although I was only moving a few minutes down the road, I was increasingly no longer in a safe or secure place in my heart. I felt incredibly alone.

My foster family were Dutch and had a grown-up son of their own who still lived at home with them. Whilst they were supportive, loving, and insistent on giving me a routine in life, I felt lost, angry and hurt. I visited my mother on occasion. She was different from how I remembered her; she seemed harder, harsher, and she was often angry. When I did visit, she locked me in my bedroom, as if it were dangerous for me to be in any other part of the house. Interpreting her mental change as something to be wary of, I, in turn, felt confused and unwanted. It's hard enough to live with strangers, but going home to visit only to be locked away fuelled a further sense of abandonment under the surface.

By this stage, my mother had found a new lover named Russell. It was clear that she was more interested in their relationship than in most other things in her life, which was ironic because the relationship was extremely violent, obsessive and destructive. Whilst I cannot speak for her, as an adult now who has studied human behaviour extensively, I understand more about why people stay in violent and destructive relationships. I recognise that the feeling of being reliable, useful, and needed, among other unconscious gains, is a strong reason to stay in a relationship, though this feeling is ultimately harmful. It appears that staying with this damaging man may have been fulfilling her need for 'purpose' at that time in her life. Perhaps it was essential for feeding her need to be included and worthwhile.

The more I saw my mother, the more tired and irritable she became. One particular memory stands out from this period in my life. She and Russell visited me at the foster home. After the visit had come to an end, we were in the back of the car saying goodbye. I had draped myself over the backseat whilst the adults were talking outside. I noticed that Russell's briefcase was open; inside were many condoms and a bundle of paperwork. I knew that the condoms were not for children, and I'd never really seen them before – they transfixed me.

When it came time for them to go, whilst the others turned away, Russell pretended to say goodbye to me and leaned in to give me a cuddle. Meanwhile, he secretly put his hand around my throat, slowly tightening his grip, and whispered in my ear, 'You were having a good look in my case then you little bitch. Who do you think you are?' I was terrified to move and terrified to say a word. I remember that fear, that breach of trust. I felt incredibly afraid. In that moment, my blood started to rush through my veins whilst it seemed simultaneously to drain away from my head. Standing there on the roadside curb with this man and his hand contracting around my throat, my senses were alert. The dampness of the road glistened on the concrete. The sounds around me, other familiar voices, were in my ears yet distant. Everything seemed to move in slow motion, but my blood was rapidly coursing and hot. He let go of me and resumed his pleasant smiles with the adults. I stumbled back. The adults were none the wiser. Together, Russell and my mother left me to stay with the Dutch family.

Not long after this incident, I was visiting my mother overnight, as was sometimes but rarely arranged by my foster parents. Despite being in charge of taking me to school, Russell had slept in, so we were late. Because of the rush, he poured my breakfast cereal without milk. He forced me to eat it dry and then proceeded to literally drag me, gripping my wrist tightly, out of the house. He tugged me along the hard surface of the road so far and so fast, always in front of me, a grimace on his face, pulling and heaving because I couldn't keep up with his frenzied pace. His long, curly, dark hair flopped around his face whilst I frantically scurried along, trying to move my legs as fast as I possibly could. I didn't have any shoes on, so my feet were bleeding by the time we arrived at the school. After what seemed like an eternity, we stopped. My feet burned incredibly hot, leaving bright red spots of blood around my toes, an external pain that mixed with a different internal feeling, a feeling of hurt that was buried deep inside my chest. I dared not show my hurt, as it only served to fuel his anger. I later found out from my mother that, not surprisingly, he had been incredibly abusive to many people in his life. He was accused of raping women with pool cues and was subsequently arrested for his crimes. Eventually, this troubled pair parted, ending the hurt and abuse suffered by all of us.

It may seem easy to blame, to point my finger and feel abused by this man's behaviour. I can absolutely say that at the time, I felt violated, hurt and confused. As an adult now, perhaps surprisingly to you, I feel no resentment. You see, I see all things from multiple sides. I know that only I can hold onto and remain with negative memories - as that's all they are now, memories. Imagine for a moment what it would take to feel the kind of rage that could cause a grown man to act this way toward a child, or indeed to anyone. I fully understand that some people may feel this rage but not act this way, regardless of the severity of their emotion. It does not excuse or condone his behaviour or my mother's for not being able to see the hurt she was exposing her small child to. It's not my place to hang onto that hurt, that emotion. If I were to hold onto it, all it would do is affect me negatively today, when these events happened so long ago.

I feel that this particular experience is an example of someone not having access or exposure to being able to identify and relate to their own feelings and emotions in a self-aware way, and consequently resorting to expressing their own hurt violently. Whilst his actions hurt others, including me, I fully suspect he hurt even more. This was just a moment in time for me. He lived and perhaps still lives with this negativity every day. Deep inside me I know this, and I would spend any time available to me to support him or anyone like him to take his emotional control back and live a life of choice and peace. Empathy without judgement - forgiveness without hate. Ultimately, it is me who feels peace inside, as that is in my control. It's a much lighter place to be.

Time moved on. My mother continued to drive her truck, my father continued to live with his girlfriend at my grandmother's house, and I went to school, continuing to live with my foster family. One particular Christmas stands out for me at the foster home, around the time I was nine years old. It was early on Christmas morning. I remember being so excited at five in the morning and waiting, waiting, waiting for the others to wake up. Finally, Pauline and Tony, my foster parents, and Dan, my foster brother, were awake and it was time to open presents! As I descended down the stairs I felt the building anticipation, the specialness of the day, until I saw the presents under the tree and noticed that many of them were still in their original packaging – not wrapped in Christmas paper. Something alerted me deep within that all was not right, and the specialness of the moment started to fade within me. My fears came true as Pauline turned to me and told me my mother had brought some presents for me. She handed me a blank card, still in its clear plastic, that had not been written in. I looked up at her with wide eyes, searching for meaning in her gesture. She said, 'I wanted you to know that your mother hasn't written in the card or wrapped your presents'. My heart sank. Not knowing the full meaning of the act, my senses picked up the essence: I wasn't worthy of effort.

As I look back at that moment today, I think about how hard it must have been for Pauline to provide the reality and not to save my mother's dignity. She must have summoned deep courage to open me up to the harsh world and tell the truth. I love her for this. You might think she should have wrapped the presents, written in the card, and pretended that all was well. But I clearly see that she did the brave thing, the right thing. She told me the truth. Not many people did that in my early years. It's only later in life that I've come to appreciate this act from her. This, in my eyes, is called integrity and being a worthwhile role model. I needed that lesson to shape my own values for my life. Goodness knows I wasn't getting it anywhere else.

As you can imagine, there were times when my confusion and angst got the better of me. I remember often being very upset around bedtime, not wanting to go to bed and feeling very alone. Being alone isn't always about not having people around you. For me, being alone was about wanting to have people on my side, to go to bat for me, to do things for me that weren't for someone else's gain but for me, for my benefit. I felt as if I had to prove myself, to be good enough, to work hard to be appreciated. Of course, this is perception and is completely constructed into my belief and value patterns through my experience of the events I was a part of. These significant emotional events in childhood extremely and deeply affected my own sense of self-worth. I developed sleepwalking problems and would wander the house at night partly naked. I was even found hanging out of a second-floor window in my sleepwalking dream state. My foster parents were clearly starting to notice the stress I was dealing with, and everyday life became harder for all of us. Their patience was starting to wane. I am sure they asked themselves, 'How long can we continue to have our own lives disrupted? When will the interruption end?' One day, my foster family took a break for a few days by themselves, and I was left behind to stay at a family friend's house for a few nights. Subconsciously, this became overwhelming for me. I wouldn't go to bed, I wouldn't eat, and I screamed and cried. My bawling became so gut-wrenching that my temporary hosts called my foster parents to come home from their holiday because I just couldn't be subdued.

With tired, angry faces, my foster parents took me home, where I continued to scream, thrash, and refuse anything and everything they tried to give me to calm me down. I sat on the stairs in the foster home until I was empty of emotion, there was nothing left to express, to expel. I simply could no longer go along with this confusing, changing world. Pauline and Tony cared for me physically and emotionally until life took its toll on me and I became a very difficult child to look after. I was no longer the easygoing, eager-to-please child. I threw tantrums and became increasingly argumentative.

Not long after these events, I was at school one day when it was time to go to the television room to watch a video. Herds of children excitedly walked in front of and around me, ready for a school treat. As I entered the warm room, everything around me started to spin. It felt almost as though I was in my very own internal whirlwind. My body started to shut down and I slowly sank to the floor and became unconscious. When I awoke, I had been taken to the washroom. I was lying on a hard wooden bench. A few people stood around me whilst the teachers called an ambulance. I have no memory of where I went or what happened next. The first thing I remember is being at my grandmother's house with my father.

My childhood doctor visited me and tested my neurological functioning. I had lost the ability to walk and my limbs had ceased responding. I was diagnosed with stress, and it was recommended that I rest and recuperate for as long as necessary in order to heal. My father, his girlfriend Sara, and my grandmother now looked after me. It was a few days before I could support myself again physically. I had been diagnosed as having a nervous breakdown, and all of a sudden, life changed once again. Now, without explanation or planning, I lived with my father.

My grandmother's home was small, warm, and very old-fashioned. She was the type of grandmother who smothers you with love and affection and who believes you can do no wrong. Perfect for my situation as an eight-year-old nervous breakdown child, wouldn't you say? My father had given up international truck driving and was now driving cement trucks locally whilst his teenage girlfriend Sara continued her life with him. With the four of us living under one roof, it felt like the adults were attempting to create some sense of normalcy. As I recovered from my stress condition in a short few days, I was relocated to a school closer to my new home. It's the funny things I remember, like the new uniform I was convinced made me look like a tree! It was a brown and green uniform, and I absolutely hated it. When I was picked up from primary school, Sara would often be the one to collect me. She always stood a long way away from the school gates, away from the other 'mums'. Overhearing a particular conversation between the adults revealed to me that gossip was definitely still rife in the community and that Sara was being shunned for her age and the inappropriateness of the circumstances she found herself in with my father. Looking back on the situation now, it seems to me that as a young adult herself, she needed protection and love from her family, who had at that time broken away from her. I've always respected Sara and felt for her. There were times as a child when I treated her as a parent and spent hours thinking she was the worst person in the world for taking my dad's attention away from me – typical child behaviour. Ultimately, though, I believe she has always been kind to me, and at a very early age I developed the ability to see from other people's points of view. I'd experienced so much in my short life; I never wanted another to feel what I had felt. I didn't need to know or understand the details of her situation, but I instinctively felt we were part of the same world, one in which pain and heartache were constant. I could see it in her eyes, a sense of sadness and a longing for inclusion. I saw in her what I felt in my heart, and this connected us deeply. I later realised, I did not judge her: I loved her.

For a short time, life was what you could call secure. My grandmother taught me to play music on her old electric organ. I took piano lessons. I invited friends from school over to tea and my father and Sara were happy. My mother was not a big part of my life at this stage, though I knew that she and her new partner Frank were getting serious as a couple. They had decided to move in together at his house, which was located in Essex, about ninety minutes drive from our family home in Kent. Because my mother was moving in with Frank, we were on the move too. The family home had become available. My mother had vacated it to move in with Frank and my father negotiated for him, Sara, and me to move back in, to have a bigger house and home. Everyone agreed and we moved back into the place where the story started.

Moving back to my old school, where I was reunited with my closer friends, was fantastic. I was also able to become close to my dearest friend Suzanne again – yes, she has the same name as me. In fact, you'll remember the neighbour my mother used to leave me with for days. Well, Suzanne was the middle child in that family. She became my protector and rock through tumultuous times. I'll share more about Suzanne later. As we settled into our new life together, my father continued to work locally, and Sara began working too. Because our house was located in the countryside, the outdoors lifestyle was always beckoning. Living right in front of a farm, my friends and I had plenty of exposure to riding horses and playing with our dogs in the fields. We spent a lot of energy discovering new places and sneaking succulent fruit into our mouths in the strawberry fields in the late summer. I felt like I belonged again, settling down into a routine after a few hectic years. My core group of friends were all girls the same age as me and there were a few who stayed at my house on weekends to play. Whilst Suzanne was three years older than me, we were always the best of friends.

I was around the age of ten when one particular night close to Christmas Sara went to a party with her workmates. My father and I were at home and my friend Lucy was also with us, which was quite normal, as she stayed over regularly on weekends. Lucy was a gregarious character, even though she was only ten years old! Coming from a family of three sisters, from a broken home, and being starved for attention, she was known for getting that attention in the most bizarre ways. On this particular evening, I remember she confided in my father that she had what she described as funny feelings in her 'fanny' (or, the proper term, vagina). My father invited her upstairs to his bedroom and asked me if I wanted to come too.

Now, you know where this is going already I'm sure. As an adult it's easy to see, but put yourself in a ten-year-olds shoes; it all just seemed like a game. I declined the invite to go upstairs because I was happy watching television. Some time passed before Lucy and my father retuned downstairs. She candidly came over to me and whispered in my ear, 'Your dad let me touch his willy!' It felt as if time was going both fast and slow at the same time. My external response was an apathetic 'whatever', as if what she was revealing was perfectly normal and I couldn't be bothered with the news. Of course, as a child, this meant very little to me on a conscious level, though what was being set up in my system was a great deal more mistrust and betrayal. This memory was only reignited when I was fifteen and again when I was in my early thirties, when I learned as an adult more about what had occurred – more of this story will come later.

Not long after these events, my beautiful grandmother passed away – on my eleventh birthday, no less. My father, my older cousin Lisa, and others from the family had been with my grandmother, as she grew more and more ill in her old age. She passed away in her hospital room at the age of sixty-eight of a heart attack. Whilst my memories are hazy as to whether I attended her funeral or not, I remember feeling a big hole in my life. It dawned on me that the safest person in my life had left me. I was never going to see her again. My grandmother always made me feel secure, like she would make the world change shape if it meant I would feel better. Her softness, loyalty, and constant belief in me were essential in my learning what it means to be part of a family and to love unconditionally.

As it does, time continued to move on. My mother re-entered my life and I was occasionally scheduled to visit her at her new house in Essex. I find it hard to explain my mother. The best way to describe her is as subtly manipulative and incredibly self-centred. Frank, her new partner, was also a truck driver, and they drove together internationally. At some point, my mother decided she wanted to be a nurse. She'd had enough of the driving lifestyle and wanted to fulfil an unrecognised passion, so she studied and became a nurse. When I visited my mother at this time in my life, she acted very paranoid. She was determined to use me, her eleven-year-old child, as a go-between for her and my father, which is a typical unconscious strategy in family break-up circumstances.

She would try to convince me that Sara and my father were purposely using washing powder that I was allergic to in order to poison me. She also warned me about my father and would frighten me by saying things about him that made me terrified to go near him. Once, she outright lied to her friends in front of me, saying that I went to boarding school, the very best school in England, and that she was so very proud of me for getting into this prestigious school. I never went there. My inner feelings were of mistrust and wariness, and it was around this time that I started to understand and learn diplomacy.

Even as a child I knew that to uncover her lies would be wrong. I knew that if someone lied and was caught out, it could cause conflict, angry faces, and shouting voices; it could cause people to be at odds with each other. So I learned to tell the truth without revealing lies. I was *eleven!* As much as she tried to convince me that my father was dangerous, she stuck up for him and then became adamant that Sara was the poison – that Sara was the one to be wary of. As you can imagine, living with my father and Sara made me confused about my mother's meaning, and I became increasingly upset and afraid of talking to her. She had become unpredictable, and I didn't know whom I could trust. One particular occasion best describes the impact her behaviour had on me.

My mother had driven me home to my father at our family home in Kent. Because they were not talking,

I was dropped at Mr and Mrs Connelly's house, three doors away from my own home. I would be dropped off there, and when my mother left, my father would come and collect me. My father arrived before my mother had left on this occasion, and from all the terror that I'd been hearing about what my father and Sara would do to me, when I saw him I screamed at the top of my lungs. I ran, a terrified child screaming with all my might. I literally fled home. I was akin to a wild animal flailing around and scared to death. My father, shocked and surprised by my outburst, raged all the way home. I could hear him shouting and storming up the street. He was furious, and I assume uncertainty was mixed with all his anger. I arrived at the house much like a trapped bird, fluttering and flailing, trying to escape his wrath. He found me and proceeded to hit at me, punching a hole in the front room's solid wooden door centimetres from my head. At this point I was sent to my room as if I had done something wrong. I screamed, cried, and fretted until I fell asleep from all the energy I had spent. He later explained he was embarrassed at my public display in the street, and I fully suspect he was confused and let his own emotions overrule logic and care.

There are many examples of these stories in my childhood. Why do I choose to tell them to you? It's not to cause shock, sadness, or upset. I don't intend for anyone to dwell on the details, and I am certain you can relate to similar feelings or events from your own experiences. I tell them because I've learned that these moments do not define me, even events from such an early age. 'How's that?' you may wonder. When I think about these times now, I see the circumstances for what they are. I see my father and my mother for who they were and the situations that led them to behave the way they did and devastate their own lives. I believe that my parents are products of their environment. They truly didn't know any better, and they had no self-awareness. Humans learn how to think, to behave, and to be, and some have more exposure to positive learning than others. Like Russell, the adults in my life to this point acted negatively because of their emotions and lack of understanding of how to interpret them. They hadn't spent time understanding what triggered them, what made them tick, what caused them to act. They simply acted without thinking of the consequences and were prone to abdicating responsibility.

Believe me, this doesn't excuse knowing right from wrong and being able to control oneself rather than harming another. But on much reflection and understanding about human beings, I accept that people become overly emotional when they don't understand themselves. If someone doesn't have purpose or have clarity in *who* they are and the power they have in controlling their lives, they will go one of two ways: they will sink and be subservient and perceive their environment as 'in control' of them, or they will lash out and damage everything around them. Knowing the backgrounds of my parents' childhoods, I know they carried their hurt and experiences throughout their lives, as did I, to a point. The difference is that I decided to break the mould, to change the anger and hurt into something positively productive. These profound changes occurred later in my life, however. I had a few more experiences to come before those lessons were learned.

A Flourishing Mind

'The world needs more people who are kind to each other. Kindness comes from understanding another's perspective. Being willing to see another human being without judgement, from extending a part of yourself to being a little vulnerable.'

Alive & Kicking Solutions

Chapter 2
In Kind

People are inherently kind; some just lose that kindness along the way. In the research for my master's degree, I have read much work on the basic drive of toddlers to want to give their possessions, food or toys to others. They want to share and they want to give. In fact, this innately kind and giving behaviour is linked to their own self-worth and happiness. Along the way, as our mind develops and we grow older, it seems that we humans can lose the simple notion of kindness at times and let cynicism and suspicion cloud our inherent giving nature. I want to introduce you to an enormously kind family. You may remember them from the previous chapter: the people that lived a few doors down the road. These were the people who looked after me when my mother left me at their house for days at a time.

Carol, the mother, has three children: Angela, Suzanne (my closest, dearest, and most important friend), and Andrew. This group of people showed me at a very early age what the meaning of true family is. As I grew older, just before I hit the teenage years, I began to spend a lot more time with Suzanne's family. Living right in front of a farm, Suzanne and I had access to a lot of space. Being older than me, she was allowed more freedom to explore than I was. I know now that Carol really saw the potential in me and that whilst her responsibility was for her own family, she impacted me greatly with her inclusion of me as another child. In fact, the whole family had an impact on me.

We lived on a country lane that had exactly twenty-seven houses on it. The lane was a thin, winding road that had a crooked red brick wall on one side protecting the woodland. On the other side of the wall, all the houses were neatly lined up alongside each other. The road was a mixture of grand houses and smaller modest ones. Our house was one of the only council houses on the road, though it certainly didn't look like a council house because of its uniqueness; it wasn't like traditional council houses, which are akin to living in a box or cage. We were lucky to live in such a lush area. Suzanne's family had made money in the automobile industry and were comfortable financially. My father, who I still lived with, was growing poorer. He had had great financial success in earlier years, but he was a slave to his emotions, which, as we know, often causes irrational decision-making, in his case with poor money management. Subsequently, he created lowly results. I was always the poor kid. I had very little pocket money, if any, and as I hung around with kids older than me, I was often judged for not being able to buy things that others were buying. I felt that I was not good enough and that to be included and respected I had to pay my own way.

My father hadn't looked after himself well, and at this stage in the late 1980s he had already had two heart attacks and was relatively unhealthy. His job paid poorly and the business he had once owned had a lot of debt. Sara worked in administration roles. I continued to attend the public school closest to us. My father drove trucks and found deals to get involved with. He was a part-time petty criminal – plain and simple. Growing up in the back streets of South East End London predisposed him to the underworld, and he continued to live the life he knew so well. If there were a way to cut a corner, make a deal, or get something for nothing, he would make it happen. He had a short stint in jail in his earlier years for holding up a post office with a sawn-off shotgun. He was a 'bother boy' in his youth and was paid to beat up people who hadn't paid the 'boss'. Violence, and what I consider heightened emotions that weren't channelled or understood, frequently ruled and fuelled him.

As the three of us settled into our new lives, my father became more and more petty and angry and even more of a bully. He was a stickler for rules. Being in control was incredibly important to him. He would set me certain tasks to be completed around the house and became incredibly strict and agitated if they were not performed to his excruciating and unrealistic standards. I was expected, and rightly so, to clean my room once a week. I was to dust, hoover, and be thorough – keep in mind that I was around twelve years old at this stage. My father would inspect my room, run his fingers along the shelves, and pick objects up and check under and around them. If he found a single inch that hadn't been properly cleaned in his eyes, he would become a hurricane in my own little world and throw things, thrash, turn the room upside down, and demand that I clean it properly!

My greatest protector, Suzanne, saw this behaviour occur often and would, whilst in his presence and in the midst of his anger, literally puff out her teenage chest and scream at him to leave me alone. She's the only person I remember ever standing up to him for me. The amazing result of her defiance was that this seemed to snap my father out of his rage and he would quickly calm down. Suzanne is the most wonderful, inclusive, family-oriented person I know, and her protection taught me to stand up. It also externally helped me to understand that what was happening at times was wrong, and I needed that protection. This wasn't my fault; his behaviour, my circumstances – they were not my fault.

Christmas time was always an interesting experience for me at this stage in my life. My father was anti-establishment and would absolutely not accept Christmas into our house most years. He sometimes let us have cards and little presents, but he was adamant that the commercial aspect of the yearly, worldwide event was not to be adhered to. On occasion, he ironically and without logical reason relented and would let us decorate the house with festive joy; perhaps he just felt more cordial some years. One year when he wasn't feeling the spirit of Christmas, Sara and I sneaked decorations into my bedroom and went wild with the sparkling promise of life – disobeying his rules and causing our own bit of anarchy.

Of course, reflecting back on my father's opinions, I understand his point of view, which he carried to his grave and I know for a fact he enjoyed the togetherness Christmas brings more and more as he got older. Every Christmas I can remember, other than the one at the foster family's house, I went to Suzanne's house for a massive dose of festive cheer. On Christmas day, Suzanne would skip down the road to get permission to take me to her house, and I would soon be enveloped in love, inclusion, and celebration. I was so entrenched in their family life that there were almost as many presents under the tree for me as for Suzanne! The tree – oh, the tree – was bigger than any human in the house. The natural fire roared and there was the smell of Christmas lunch in the air, lights twinkling, and a family feel all around. Their family friends and even extended family would also include me, and one year, to my great surprise and awe, their family friend Frank, who I loved and adored, bought me my very own Swatch watch. Looking at my gift, with its shiny new bright blue strap and white clock face, whilst sitting by the tree with all the family, I was just happy to be there. I really couldn't have cared less whether there were presents at all.

Sitting near the tree, I couldn't believe it when the name Suzanne was read out, that it was meant for me. I even took the present and handed it to my friend Suzanne. The family all laughed and shook their heads. 'No', they insisted. 'This one is for you.' This was a moment to behold, a moment that said unconsciously to me as a child that I had been thought of, included, and regarded. I doubt that Frank knows to this day how much that gesture meant to me, considering other experiences at Christmas with my foster family as a benchmark. I have been very privileged to be able to express to my friend Suzanne and her family how much their support and love cradled me in my childhood. They understand the severity of my then difficult circumstances and to this day support and love me like a family member. You may think you have to do something substantial to make a difference – that you have to find a cure for cancer or spend twenty hours a week volunteering. In reality, even the smallest act, the smallest token of a word, phrase, or moment, can change someone's life. Never underestimate the power you have to make a difference.

Horses were a great part of my life. My mother is exceptional with horses and, having grown up with them, has a unique gift, along with her four sisters. The girls of the family who owned the nearby farm had grown up and moved away. Leaving their childhood horses without caretakers, the farm family gave Suzanne responsibility for one of the horses, and we spent many hours learning to ride, caring for the horse, and living the active outdoors lifestyle. The lessons I learned about completing tasks and taking responsibility were born here; to care for another living thing, especially an animal is a great honour. They relied on Suzanne and me to keep them warm and fed.

As I grew into my teens, with Suzanne being a few years older, we spent more and more time together. We were like two peas in a pod. Increasingly, I stayed at Suzanne's house overnight, whilst my father's focus remained largely on his life with Sara – they had become engaged. My mother continued to live with her new partner, Frank, whom I visited on a fairly ad hoc basis.

I was craving more freedom, and I was allowed it with Suzanne's family. They provided me a sense of normalcy. When they went out to parties or dinner, they often included me as one of their own. Suzanne even shared her pocket money and paid for my meals when we went to the local sweet shop or hung out with her friends in the town centre. She never flinched at sharing with me – such was her generosity. One year Carol even asked my father permission to pay for and take me on holiday to Greece with them, which my father flatly refused. They also wanted to take me to festive parties and fancy dress occasions, which my father also wouldn't allow me to attend. Looking back, I believe he was threatened by their acceptance of me, which in turn reflected on him and the lack of involvement and capacity he was able to give me.

Turning thirteen was a turning point in my life, not only because it signified the beginning of my teenage years, but also because I realised the capacity of my own decision-making power. I became more independent. Learning to abide by my father's instructions to satisfy his petty and stifling rules, I was ready to find ways to pay my own way. I started to work regularly at the local fish and chip shop, which was fifteen minutes walk from my family home. I worked two nights a week and on Saturday evenings, earning cash; it was my first taste of true independence. This working experience to this day has a soft spot in my heart. The owners were incredibly kind and loved having me as an employee. They were a couple, the husband a fiery Spanish man and the wife a local woman, and they had young children. Working was an escape for me where my stifling life at home seemed far away and I was respected and given responsibility.

I thoroughly enjoyed putting on my red and white striped apron and red hat, enthusiastically getting into the lively jovial character. I was a fast, accurate and hilarious version of me, behind the serving counter. Putting on clothes is just like wearing a mask, becoming an identity, another version of our own unexplored beliefs and playing a role is just the same. We humans do this every day. We get to play a character, assume a new identity and allow ourselves to contribute in different ways by taking on this new manner. The mask as a fish and chip shop girl enabled me to contribute and feel worthwhile. Be a good person, and a worthy investment of time in the owner's eyes. More than twenty people queued for their fish and chips on the busiest days, where I would become the life and soul of the party entertaining people as they ordered. Helping them to feel engaged and included. Of course, at the age of thirteen I didn't realise that this is what I was enabling, I just loved having positive attention and was grateful to be independent. I was acknowledged as being good, capable and worthy, something that to this point I only received externally away from the family unit. At school I was well regarded by my teachers, my friends parents thought I was a good influence despite the fact my life at home was unknowingly to them, turning into something of a prison.

My father and Sara were happy together, smoking, sitting in watching television and living a life of simply existing. My responsibilities grew as did I, and cleaning my room became the least of my chores. Washing dishes, cleaning the house, picking up the dog poo in the garden and ironing all the clothing became something I was expected to do. I was a little workhorse at my father's beck and call at times. I attended high school, worked ten hours a week at the fish and chip shop, all whilst keeping the house for the most part. If at any stage these tasks were not completed to the standard or satisfaction of my father, then there would be punishment. I was often grounded, told off and refused treats of which I felt I had worked hard for and was promised. Of course, Suzanne the protector was on duty for a lot of this time and negotiated, persuaded and rescued as part of her role. As was Sara often trying to appeal to my Dad's softer side. It seems that for a large part of his life, my father seemed to be out of control. He himself abused as a child and knowing only mostly force, brute force at that. His own father was a harsh man, always expecting better, more. My father protected his younger sister often as a child and young woman, he had a protective streak, and a very kind heart. He just lost his way, getting carried away and forgetting this kinder side of his own identity at times. Stuck in the habit of anger.

A massive accomplishment occurred when I saved enough money to buy my own CD player. They were new at the time and I really, really wanted one. After I bought it, I took it into my bedroom and set it up. My father was incredibly proud of me for saving and buying something with my wages. It was such a proud moment in my life. My very first CD was an Elton John album (yes, I know; I was a teenager, wise beyond my years!). Playing his songs and hearing the words of the song 'Daniel' whilst sitting in my bedroom alone brought me into floods of tears. I was meant to be happy, to be proud. I wasn't. I was still lonely and felt like a single fragment of a body, broken and isolated. Really, I just had a new CD player; it wasn't what I wanted deep inside.

Because I was with Suzanne constantly and exposed to her friends, I acted older than I was, and at thirteen years old I met my first teenage love, Gary. He was eighteen. Our crowd of people were at the age where cars were starting to enter into our lives. After walking around the town and countryside up to this point in our lives, cars gave us much greater freedom. With not much to do in a small town, driving around and meeting friends in car parks to hang out, listen to music, and let the teenage hormones flow was all we dreamed about. Gary was a good-looking guy in my eyes. He was every teenage girl's dream, and I thought about him night and day. Nothing else existed in my world once I'd met him.

At the age of thirteen I lost my virginity to Gary. We were in his house (not to worry: I'm not going to be that explicit!) and after fooling around and being very intimate I decided it was time to go all the way and have intercourse. The song playing on his radio was the Ghostbusters theme song; yes, I had sex for the first time to the Ghostbusters theme song – not my proudest moment, perhaps, but a milestone all the same! Having sex seemed very natural to me, and I enjoyed the attention. We were not very discrete, often having sex in his bed, pretending we were lying under the covers fully clothed whilst watching the television, secretly having sex. On one occasion his sister walked in and started talking to us right at the pivotal moment, but she was none the wiser – we were that good at hiding!

The fun and games were over pretty soon when on Christmas Eve at my family home, Sara came home from work earlier than expected whilst Gary and I were taking part in my new-found hobby. We were on the floor in the front room of the house, stark naked. I heard the key in the door and I think I felt the biggest surge of panic and adrenalin I had ever felt up to that point in my life. Like a stunned animal in the headlights, I froze. Gary managed to get his trousers on and sit on the sofa at lightning speed. I, on the other hand, was struggling to get my jeans on and didn't make it in time. Sara walked through the door and with a shocked expression that soon turned to pain, she recognised what was happening. Her eyes seemed to drop and, if I were to guess, a sense of conflict came over her.

Gary was sent home and I was to await my father coming home to deal my pending punishment. Naturally, as you've probably already guessed, this wasn't a joyous occasion, and my father erupted into a furious tirade of anger. My immediate punishment was that I was to be grounded for nine whole months. School, work, and home were to be my only destinations. I was forbidden to see Gary and our relationship was broken up. My father contacted Gary's father and told him of the illegal act his son had taken part in: according to the law, the rape of a minor. All along, Gary's family were under the impression that I was fifteen and just about to turn sixteen. They were very angry and disappointed in our behaviour, and they were scared for their son, who was now facing an infuriated father who had every right to take the matter to the police. Life is ironic, isn't it?

After calming down, my father decided not to report Gary and agreed with his parents that we were never to see each other again. I was devastated. Not only was I confined to the house for nine months, a rule my father stayed true to, but I had also lost my boyfriend. I recall a photo, taken the next day, of Suzanne and me with Christmas hats. I looked terrible. I had tears running down my face and was trying to force a smile. I wasn't even allowed to go with Suzanne for our usual Christmas fun. What seemed too short a time after the break-up with Gary, he was on his merry way dating someone his own age, and I was outraged how quickly he seemed to forget me and move on. This added to my deepening despair and I once again felt very disconnected from the world.

Unbeknown to me, this punishment would later fuel my sexual appetite and rampage of men across the country. Finally, after what seemed an eternity, I was allowed my freedom once again. I joined my friends outside of school and my job. As I continued into my teens, I found a lot of solace in friendship. I always had the gift of attracting people by positive means rather than starting conflict with them. At school, as you will know, people often hang out in groups and clusters. I have always been able to act as a chameleon and merge into groups of all types. In high school, I was never bullied (there was more than enough of that at home), the teachers were respectful, my friends were accepting and inclusive, and I started to feel happier than I had in a long time. Gary was well behind me. Whilst I wasn't a super-genius at school and didn't achieve the best grades, I was average and very accepting of the fact. Just *being* was good enough for me. My appetite for boys continued to thrive, and still at the tender age of thirteen I flirted and became frisky with lots of boys, continuing to have sex with people I knew well for fun and comfort, allowing these boys to experience their first sexual encounters with me, taking for myself a sense of comfort in the act.

At school one day, the same friend who had gone upstairs with my father that night when we were ten approached me with another friend of ours, asking if she could talk to me. She explained that there was something she had to admit: that my dad had touched her. She asked me if I remembered. Up to that point, I had never specifically recalled that night until she mentioned it again, and my memories quickly came back. She said she'd felt really bad about it and worried that telling me would affect our friendship. I explained to her that it would never break up our friendship and that I was sorry it had happened. It was a short conversation, but with heavy ramifications. Later that night I confronted my father, telling him what she had said. He laughed out loud and asked me if I was all right. He said that something like that was hard to hear and that of course he hadn't done it. I asked him again and he absolutely denied it. Troubled, I left it at that and stored the experience deep inside my subconscious.

I continued to work in the fish and chip shop, where I met many people in our small town. Along came Jason. I had turned fifteen when Jason, the gamekeeper at the grounds near my house, entered my life. He was twenty-one and very sexy. Being in the outskirts of the rural side of Kent, there were beautiful manors and properties where pheasants, partridges, and the like were hunted, killed and sold. As a common practice in stately manors, gamekeepers were employed to look after the lands, birds and equipment. This is what Jason did. He would regularly come to get his dinner dressed in work trousers, long working boots, a belt to hold his trousers up, and his bare chest and muscles free for all to see. He was a tall, lean, muscular man with fair sandy hair, and after a hard day's work he had a rugged, dirty look. I flirted with him madly.

Everyone at the shop wanted me to go with his friend, who was decidedly more buff, but I wanted Jason, and when I want something, I get it. It's safe to say we got together, and I was besotted with him. It was romantic; he absolutely doted on me and I was just as obsessed with him. I stayed at his house (often pretending to be at Suzanne's house). Even my father eventually accepted him and got used to having him around. Because his work required him to be up at odd hours, I would accompany him in his four-wheel drive, keeping him company and distracting him with outdoor kissing, sex, and general naughtiness. His dog, Feet, was his pride and joy. Of course, a springer spaniel is crucial for a gamekeeper; as Jason often commanded his dog to his feet, her name became just that: 'Feet'. I met Jason's mother and felt very at home with her. The family owned a pub in Middlesex (hours from where we lived), and even though I was fifteen (for real this time), they were just happy their son was happy.

As life was settling down, it was time to decide on my future. My father and Sara were still not in a financial position to write home about, and my mother was married to Frank and living a settled life of her own in Essex. After talks with everyone it was decided that going to college and furthering my education was the best option, which meant going to live with my mother and Frank. Jason promised he would visit me often and when I finished school, I had a massive party at my family home at which I said an earnest goodbye to my friends, family, Suzanne and Jason. The higher education part of my life was upon me, and moving to my mother's seemed a good option. The college I was destined to attend was well respected, and when I visited, it seemed friendly and interesting. After the move, I settled in with my mum and Frank. Frank was an incredibly nice man; he looked somewhat like Richard Gere with his grey hair and pointed facial features and was from Manchester in the north of England. He was possibly the kindest parental figure I encountered in my life. He had no children and took me on like one of his own – even though I wasn't so much the child anymore. I had grown up and become incredibly attractive, with my sculpted, blooming body attracting men left, right, and centre.

Whilst I was waiting for the college term to start, I spent weeks on my own in the house, waiting for my mum to come home from work, bored. Frank was away driving weeks at a time, and being new in the area, I had absolutely no friends. One day my mother invited me to go to the hospital where she worked. She requested I wear a particular dress and shoes that made me look gorgeous and very grown up. When I arrived and found her, she unashamedly paraded me around, looking at me with self-importance and introducing me to her colleagues. As usual, I felt like a puppet, though the attention and seeming admiration from my mother was welcome. Conversely, the underlying gloating about this pretty thing she'd produced was almost sickly and overwhelming. I remember how the men she introduced me to would look me up and down and make funny comments to my mother like 'She couldn't possibly have come from you', with everyone chuckling and playing along.

It became normal for her to tell lies right in front of me. The most common lie was that I went to boarding school, and this untruth came up there in the hospital in front of her colleagues. I was feeling increasingly lonely and alienated in this new world with no-one to talk to, no-one to share experiences with, and certainly no-one I felt I could trust. I became obsessed with my looks, as my appearance seemed to be the thing that attracted the most attention. I was the lowest weight I'd ever been and looked very healthy and toned. I even started to prance around the grimy, dirty concrete streets of Essex trying to get attention in revealing clothes, not quite the kind of revealing attire the millennium years have achieved great heights with, but tight-fitting, almost classic long lines, with slits in the skirts and well-formed tops that left little to the imagination, showcasing my glorious, perky young figure.

After a couple of months living with my mother, my life felt empty and dull. Jason visited me a couple times, and these visits were a deep relief to my ever-growing discomfort and boredom. My mother adored him, and as you might imagine, with her insatiable need to feel needed and wanted she flirted with him constantly. In fact, as I grew older I realised that whilst my father had been the one to play around and flirt, my mother wasn't far from following the same path. Going back in my memory to when I spent a lot of time with her in the truck travelling Europe as a child, I remember a distinct time when we were in Spain and Derek, one of the other truck drivers, was co-driving with her. There were bunk beds in the massive cabs that were used for sleeping when it was time to stop driving.

When it was starting to get late, we had supper at a stunning little Spanish bar where the locals were infatuated with calling me *bella* and pinching my chubby little cheeks. Whilst getting ready for bed, my mother turned to me and asked, 'Would you mind if mummy slept with Derek?' Of course, as a small child, this didn't mean much to me, though there was a tiny little feeling of disappointment and shame. I knew inside myself that this behaviour wasn't normal, as other children didn't report their mothers asking them these types of questions. Whilst I may not have been intellectually aware or developed enough mentally to understand the intricacies of adult monogamy or relationships, I could compare the sorts of stories and feelings others at my age were expressing, and mine were different, very different. Typically, as I'd learned to do, I switched on my apathetic mode and shrugged my shoulders to indicate that I didn't care. As you can imagine, as I got older and understood more about adult relationships, I realised what must have been taking place right above me in the top bunk.

Back in Essex, due to the constant boredom and increasing loneliness and being miles away from my dearest friends and allies, I decided I couldn't possibly wait any longer to see Jason and planned a trip on the train to visit him in Hampshire. With permission from my mother to spend five days with him, I was ready to have an adventure!

A Flourishing Mind

'Thousands of candles can be lit from a single candle, and the life of the candle will not be shortened. Happiness never decreases by being shared.'

Buddha

Chapter 3
Beyond You

It was never my intention to stay for long in Hampshire while visiting – it just happened. As with any decision, there were consequences. You see, I was fifteen years old and could taste freedom in getting away from my parents. They weren't good for me and I inherently knew it. It was summertime in England when I got on the train from my mother's town in Essex. The warmth of the air and the excitement of going on a trip by myself to see my lover was overwhelming. The sense of liberty was setting in.

The trip from Essex to Hampshire was almost two hours on the train and a fairly easy journey, with a changeover in busy London. Setting off alone with my small bag of clothes and my ticket in hand, I started what was unknowingly to me about to become one of the defining moments of my life. Spending time with Jason was all I had dreamed about while in Essex. I just wanted to see him and feel appreciated and loved – his attention was all encompassing. A shy person himself, I found that he needed me in a different way to others. I was a drug to him, not a chess piece, like my parents seemed to use me as. Five days away from Essex seemed like bliss, and our time together during my short stay was perfect. I saw the magnificent countryside of Hampshire in a little village called Grately with a population of approximately one hundred people. It was a small town and I was excited to see its charming beauty. The nearest town to the small village was Andover. Let me help you get your bearings. You may know where Stonehenge is. Well, Andover is about twenty minutes away.

The house Jason was staying in was on its own private lake. The off-white house with expansive grounds was as if out of a fairy tale. Its living room looked out upon the lake, where pink and white water lilies floated whilst the ducks and other wildlife meandered on by. A small, old brick bridge connected the main house, where the landlady lived, to the staff living quarters a few metres on the other side of the bridge. Whilst Jason wasn't staff at this particular house, this was the only room available for him.

Beyond the boundary of the little white house lay thatched cottages with winding roads that connected the countryside to the villages, where farmers, shopkeepers, and the like lived out their lives in a simple and peaceful way. This lifestyle beckoned to me. Roaming around in a red pickup truck, being with Jason where the only expectation was to love and to make love, I had found my heaven on Earth. Five days soon passed and it was time to return to the streets of Essex, where manipulation, expectation, and confusion were waiting and lingering like a bad odour. With many tears, hurt in my heart, and stalled attempts at leaving this paradise, I clung to Jason. I begged him to let me stay, but with a heavy heart I finally and reluctantly boarded the train to return home.

The journey to Essex was excruciating. The tears continued to fall down my face and I knew that going 'home' was futile, that it was not a safe place for me. Much like my experience as an eight-year-old when my body shut down from the stress, I knew I was feeling grief and loss. I truly wanted to escape the drama and the hold my parents had over my life. It was clear to me; even though I was perhaps unable to articulate it clearly, the feeling and inner knowing of some core instinct was apparent. If I stayed with my parents, I would be stuck in a place physically and emotionally harmful. I faced fight or flight. If I went back, my potential was diminished. If I stayed with Jason I would have a chance to make my own decisions.

As with most trains, we stopped at major junctions, unloading and loading new passengers who were travelling their own journey. My train rolled into Basingstoke, a beautiful city in the west of England. People were getting on and off the train, on and off, on and off. Without any hesitation, thought, or conscious awareness, my legs suddenly began to move, slowly at first, and then with a rush of heat and adrenalin. I realised I was leaving the train with my bag and entering the platform, joining other passengers as they went about their lives, none of us knowing that this single action had just created a major and life-changing turn for me.

People rushed all around me on the platform as I stood like a deer in headlights, wide-eyed, scared, and desperately trying to figure out what to do next. The sun was moving over the station into the midday heat, and I felt the beginnings of sweat start to trickle down my back. Standing in my pretty red summer dress, I noticed a telephone box nearby. The station was becoming quite golden from the sun as I searched for the coins I needed to make the telephone call to Jason so I could tell him I'd gotten off the train. Entering the telephone box with a shaking body, I trembled as I dialled his number, hoping desperately that he would be home and available to take the call from the communal area of his quarters. He answered the phone and I quickly explained where I was and what I had done, and that I didn't really know what I was going to do next.

There was dismay in Jason's voice, and the fact that he was telling me to get back on the train and go home was terrifying. I knew he was saying this because he wanted what was best for me: going home, staying out of trouble, and going to college like I was supposed to. This wasn't enough for me; it only told me what I couldn't do, and I had had enough of that mindset. I wanted more freedom. I wanted my own life, to be away from the darker manipulation that beckoned if I returned to where I had come from. I had a sudden realisation that this was really happening. I had taken an incredibly major step to stand up for myself, and I felt that the notion of travelling home was gone, lost and irretrievable. I had created a chance for myself, a chance to live my life my way, and no-one was going to stop me.

A Flourishing Mind

It was getting hotter in the little telephone box. Perspiration saturated my entire body and my clothing, making it harder to think and extremely uncomfortable. I declared to Jason that I was going to go back to him and asked him to pick me up at the station at the same place he had left me only hours before.

Whilst travelling all the way back to Hampshire, watching the familiar scenery speed by, I fretted about whether Jason would be there. My actions, thoughts, and feelings all started to seem very surreal. My worry started to trump my bravery, and apprehension started to take hold. I was nervous and living so much in the present that I lost most of my rational mind. I was living on pure emotion, forgoing any past or present notion of the very consequences I mentioned before. As the train rolled into the station, Jason's trusty red pickup truck was waiting, as was he in his dirty boots, with his tanned body and a face that told me he was afraid. All I felt was relief! Jason was worried and knew that these actions spelled trouble. He told me that there was still time to go back. Perhaps not knowing the events of my past propelled him to assume that I was safe, or even that I was prone to exaggeration, but he respected my firm decision and took me back to his home. Driving back to his house, the adrenalin surged through my veins. Finally, after what seemed an eternity, I was getting out of his car and walking back over the familiar bridge past the little white house. Walking into his quarters, I started to feel calmer; I knew Jason would take care of me. I thought I would live with him. Jason knew this wouldn't be possible, and I was about to find out why.

The landlady of the house was an old, white-haired woman who lived alone. I remember looking in through her window once, walking through the pretty gardens and seeing the luxurious house she had lived in all her life. Being a modern and somewhat forthright girl of the 1990s I realised quickly that she and I had very different values. Having never met her before, it was quite a shock when she saw me talking with Jason in the staff quarters and rushed over in her floating, airy garments like something out of a fantasy fairy movie, screaming at me to get out: 'You will leave! You are not welcome here and will not stay in this house, you hussy!' Jason seemed to be expecting this and didn't appear surprised. I later found out that my five-day stay with him was somewhat under the radar and was against the house rules. The landlady had never twigged I was there, and I was kept a secret. I was quite promptly marched out of the premises and abruptly seated in Jason's car, ready to be deported from her house. Jason followed and calmed her down with his good-boy charming nature. She trusted he would do the right thing and not take advantage of her by letting me stay in his rooms.

Sitting in the passenger seat of his car, I knew this wasn't ideal and that I had inadvertently caused a domino effect of drama in my and Jason's worlds. He needed to get back to work, to looking after the game in the fields of Grately and its surroundings, so I decided to accompany him, as I had many times before, thinking we would find a way to stay together as we roamed the countryside in tandem. Knowing I had to alert my mother that I was not coming home, we stopped at a random telephone box at the side of the winding country road, where I explained this very fact. My mother's reaction was precisely what I expected: she was shocked, angry, and defensive. It seems never to have occurred to her to come to Hampshire to collect me. In fact, I was simply left there, and perhaps this was a silent but welcome relief to us all.

My father wasn't much in my life at this point except for rare telephone conversations because he was happy with Sara, who had grown into a professional woman, and they enjoyed each other's company. I do recall a feeling that my father trusted me and knew I could handle myself. Whilst I don't explicitly remember how I told him I wasn't coming home to him or my mother, I don't recall whether he ever sought me out. Thinking about this now as an adult, it seems quite surprising that neither of my parents came to get me, their fifteen-year-old daughter who was now living on her own with her trusted boyfriend without any income or support. Sure, I was street-smart from the countless journeys to Europe in the truck driving years before, being in charge of reading foreign maps and negotiating with customs officials through the glass windows of docking areas in various different countries. I thought that surely someone would come and see if I was all right, invited or not.

This is where the chapter heading, *Beyond You*, takes hold. I find and have found throughout my life that people have the capacity to see beyond themselves, though they don't always exercise this ability. At times, we all see others in need or recognise that there is something in the world that would benefit from our attention that perhaps isn't directly related to our own personal gain. Seeing and knowing this, we often still turn a blind eye. We look the other way and apathetically expect another person or entity to deal with the issue. Neither of my parents saw beyond themselves at this stage, either. When I put myself in their shoes, though, I can see why. I was very capable and assertive, and since I had Jason, perhaps they believed this was a good chance for me, an opportunity for me to take the lead in the life I wanted and relieve the burden I may have been in their worlds. They were both lost in their own lives. Of course, I'm sure they loved me in their own way. I suspect, and truly it is my perception, that they felt I was safe. I was with Jason and they left me to my own decisions.

The wonderful turn of events that was about to happen, whilst admittedly difficult at the time, showed me that whilst my parents didn't particularly act beyond themselves, total strangers did, and those strangers saved my life.

Having very limited living options in Hampshire, my life soon became an adventure. I would sneak into Jason's room every night after dark hoping the white witch wouldn't stumble upon me. Jason was petrified that he would get caught and pleaded with me to go home. But having tasted decision-making and the freeing feeling of independence, I wasn't going anywhere. One sunny day, the landlady caught sight of me and turned her wrath once more in my direction. By this time, I had experienced her nature and was ready to use my diplomacy and negotiation skills to the fullest. Talking to her calmly and rationally, I lied through my pretty little teeth and claimed to be only visiting in the daytime, promising that no night-time sleepovers were occurring.

The white witch's argument was that I was taking up residence without her consent and that even if the visits were only during the day, I should be paying rent for that time. So, ingeniously, I offered Jason's services as rent payment and suggested he paint her staff quarters for free! I promised again that I wouldn't stay overnight and she begrudgingly agreed. I was very proud of myself and thought myself very clever for throwing her off-guard until Jason had painted the quarters. Eventually, I was discovered at night in his room by her spying male friend and unashamedly thrown off her property. And so, a week into my new exciting life, I found myself homeless.

I walked the country streets in the daytime, waiting for Jason to swing by and pick me up whilst he worked, as I continued to accompany him on his rounds. In the moments along the way, I pondered where to live and how to survive in my new unfounded world. Thankfully, the air was warm even at night, and I found myself sleeping in Jason's car and in fields, waiting for the next day to come so I could see and be with him. Being a country village, there wasn't much work, so I ventured on the train to Andover, only a few miles from the village, to begin my quest for work. It quickly occurred to me that not having a phone number or address for applications was a detractor for potential employers.

I can't say I was unhappy with this new life. I was free from all the drama and manipulation of my parents, so being without a home and living from moment to moment was exciting and freeing. It wasn't what you might imagine; it wasn't sleeping rough on the streets whilst starving and freezing to death. Others may have had that experience, but I certainly didn't. Having said that, people didn't seem to believe in me when applying for jobs. Whilst I presented myself well, they turned me away when I couldn't provide personal details for them to contact me. I didn't find this to be a deterrent. Using my ever-reliable problem solving capabilities, I told employers I'd do the legwork and that I would pop back in tomorrow to get the results of the interview. 'I'll come to you!' I said. 'No, sorry', they said. 'That just won't work', they continued, and it obviously just wasn't how things were done. Whilst this didn't dissuade me, my courage still prevailed, as I'd always been able to look after myself up until then, hadn't I? I just had to keep going.

Some evenings, Jason would take me to the local pub. It was a massive and beautiful building that sat on a stream and had vast old walls that dated back thousands of years. Moss and ivy grew up the walls and pretty flowers with many colours surrounded it. The bartender and owner of the pub was Canadian and had lived in the area a very long time. She was a spritely lady with long, flowing, curly hair that reached her waist. She always wore part of it up in a clip and let the rest cascade down her back. One evening, knowing my situation, she kindly offered to have telephone messages and mail sent to her pub so that no-one needed to know I didn't have anywhere to live. She was a clever, kind and thoughtful genius! With a new strategy in play, I applied for more jobs, putting down her address and number as planned, and every evening I strode to her pub to collect messages and mail. No more than twenty-four hours had passed before I was asked for a second interview at a sports store in Andover's main street. Having worked at the fish and chip shop and a few other small jobs in my life up to then, I was well-qualified to work as a full-time sales assistant earning ninety pounds a week. I suitably impressed the manager, Julie, and her assistant, Donna, and was asked to start the very next day. It's a funny notion, isn't it? I couldn't get work because I didn't have an address, and I couldn't get an address because I didn't have any money. Who would have thought that this kind Canadian lady in a pub was the key to my moving forward? I wonder if she ever realised the impact she had on my life.

Needing my own belongings – more than just a bag of clothes that would last five days – Jason and I ventured back to Essex in his car to collect my possessions. Feeling more secure with a job that paid my living expenses, it was a great relief to be going home to collect my things and put an end to my days with my mother in Essex. My college application had been withdrawn and my mother had all my belongings ready in black bin bags; I had given her advance warning earlier that week. The return visit with Jason was short-lived and consisted of an angry exchange of hurtful words from both of us. Frank stood with my mother on one side of the carport, and Jason and I were on the other. We were divided. My mother's face, which was contorted with rage, and my own angry pointing finger thrust in her direction. I accused and blamed her, saying all the things I had always wanted to, perhaps not in any coherent or productive manner. It was over, I was free, and there was no going back. I don't think she wanted me back, so the feeling was mutual.

Returning to Hampshire triumphant and righteous, I began my new job at the sports store selling trainers, running shoes, balls, rackets and equipment – items I had never used before in my life. In the first week, I earned my first proper weekly wage and was presented with a small brown envelope with more cash than I had seen in a long time. When the old man who owned the sports store franchise presented me with the folded currency, I felt more alive and in control than ever. I was rewarded for my effort and persistence, and I wanted more. Now that I had funds, I could find my own place to live, so I went about searching for a room of my own, paid for on my very own. I failed to mention that I had absolutely lied about my true age of fifteen to anyone who crossed my path. Of course, to everyone else, I was eighteen, and I looked every bit that age, so my false claim was accepted without question or demands for evidence.

After buying my first newspaper, I began the search to find a place to live. There were many options to choose from and lots of rooms available for rent within my price range. Choosing my favourite advert, which claimed that I would receive one week's worth of a small room in exchange for fifty pounds, I set out to meet the owner of the house. I arrived at a small block of flats in the middle of the town, which was quite near the shop I was working in. It was late in the afternoon and heading into early evening. The sun was setting and I had come straight from work.

I remember the lady in her fifties who answered the door with a kind smile as she welcomed me into her home. She and her husband were looking for someone to help them pay their mortgage and take their spare room. They offered me the room immediately and after a few basic questions were happy to take me on. Looking at them with honest and open eyes, I offered my only fifty pounds to this lady. I explained that it was all I had and that I intended to stay but everything depended on whether I kept my job and could continue to pay weekly. Let's pause here to look back on this situation. Let's pretend I am the owner of the house – the woman who answered the door. I see a fifteen-year-old girl pretending to be eighteen standing on my doorstep and looking quite innocent. I see someone who needs help and support, and I want to help. I mean, this could be my daughter, and it makes me question how she ended up here with only fifty pounds and a bag of clothes. I believe this is what she saw, as her next gesture indicated.

The woman turned to me and said, 'You can stay for two weeks for that amount of money, and I'll include your food as well'. I hadn't even seen the room yet, but I was sold. I needed a woman who would be this kind and generous to me as much as I needed a room to sleep in. I saw the room later that night. It was terribly small – I could hardly fit my bag in it – and all it had was a single bed and curtains for privacy. Even so, I entered my new house with a sense of security and satisfaction, regardless of the size of the room. That very evening I had lots of washing to do and the kind landlady, whose name I cannot remember, helped me. I had accidentally dyed all my white washing blue. She worked with me to settle in. But whilst she and her husband settled in for a night in front of the TV, the feeling of loneliness once again came knocking at my door. I may have had a job, a place to live, and the ability to see Jason on my own terms, but with the battle finished and everything in place, once I stopped fighting there was nothing to fight for anymore. I felt lost.

Jason continued to work at his job whilst I became more competent and happy in my own work. My contribution to the household in which I lived was supporting the owner with cleaning the house as a thank you and something I could give back to her. Not knowing the concept of the law of reciprocity at that time, I realise now that I wanted to return the favour of her kindness. She was, of course, going beyond herself, unconsciously becoming a role model for me. And even though my connection with her was short-lived, her support and kindness has gone a long way toward shaping my core values. In fact, as a mature adult, I have in turn extended my home and my time to those in need, with her often in my mind.

Not many weeks had gone by when Jason was unexpectedly offered a house as part of his job. Gamekeepers often lived on the property at which they worked, though this wasn't possible with his current job, so when a bigger house became free in the village, Jason's employer took hold of the rental lease as another option for his living arrangements and Jason was moved into it. Now that he was finally away from the white witch landlady, we could live together away from her rules and with much more freedom, living in our own house, rent-free for me no less. Once again on the move, I packed my bag of clothes and happily moved in with Jason to a white two-bedroom house on Railway Parade in Grately. The house was amongst a row of six other houses situated right in front of the railway platform. I had easy access to the town and not much more than a ten-minute train ride to work every day.

Living with Jason was amazing at first and, of course, different from staying overnight on the odd occasion. We now had to contend with domestic life and sorting out our morals and rules, which being young, were unconscious for us both. Values and beliefs are created over time. We filter information and subjectively create our own meaning, and as two young people we were still getting in touch with our own personal standards and values. It's safe to say we were sorting out our own rules of cohabitation.

Finally sixteen, I was very much a legal adult to some degree, though the law was still restrictive until I was eighteen. So eighteen is what I pretended I was. Some months had passed and Jason was becoming more withdrawn, taking his dog with him everywhere and seeming to rely on her for contentment. I know this sounds strange, but he became increasingly dependent on the dog, as she was totally loyal to him whereas I was growing wings, exploring the world, and meeting new friends. He retreated to relying on the animal for companionship. Jason was shy and enjoyed the hermitic life. I was totally different: I wanted to go out, have fun, and taste all the free life had to offer. We argued more as time went on, spent more of our days apart, and began to drift away from each other with tormented hearts that were not ready to release each other.

It was then that I met Emma. Emma was a thirty-something, crazy, unleashed human being. With dramatic, dark, straight hair that was cut severely into a bob, she was pale-skinned and had piercing blue eyes. She was like people I'd only ever seen in the movies, completely independent and unrestrained. She worked at the travel agency near the sports shop and lived at her parents' house, two doors down the street from where Jason and I were living. We'd see each other at the train station every morning waiting for the train, giving each other steely looks as we crossed paths. Perhaps in our unconscious engagement we were worldly competitors, female against female in this small town. This went on morning after morning until one day the universe decided we were meant to meet one evening at the local pub. She'd had enough to drink to introduce herself, and from that moment on, we became the best of friends. I hadn't had this kind of female companionship since I had last seen Suzanne, which seemed like many moons ago. Her girly attention and gossiping ways were attractive to me and I wanted to be around her all the time – I felt like I had a new lease on life.

Every night we would frequent the pub, meeting new young people who were also local. Jason didn't come along very much. He preferred to stay at home watching TV with his dog. Being fairly self-sufficient, it didn't occur to me at the time to include him or that we were really very different people drifting apart. You could almost say I didn't really give him a second thought. In all truth, I had begun to use him and take him for granted. When I look back, it's easy to see why I treated him the way I did. I wanted to be in control and not allow another person to let me down. I was finding people who were enamoured with me and slowly ditching Jason, sensing that our relationship was waning. It's still not something I'm proud of, as the poor man didn't deserve it, though I extend forgiveness to myself and recognise the parts we both played in the demise of our relationship.

Emma and I became thick as thieves, taking on the world and all its possibilities together. She taught me new and exciting things about the world. Hearing stories of her life and her travels gave me something to aspire to. Having been restrained by the rules and petty structure created by my father for most of my life, the opposite extreme of being totally free was so appealing that I drove myself into a dangerous world of drugs and sex. Emma, being older, was wiser to how people are and shielded me from the true dangers whilst encouraging me to taste the bitter sweetness of excitement and danger. As I was increasingly leaving Jason behind, I began to experiment, teasing men with my flirting tactics and using marijuana to get high.

Emma and I were increasingly attracted to each other in sexual ways, and I soon had my first sexual encounter with a woman. One evening, we were high on pot and had been drinking at the pub. The evening had consisted of rowdy behaviour with the local boys and we had gone back to my house on Railway Parade.

In the darkness of the downstairs living room, whilst Jason lay in our bed upstairs, Emma and I began to kiss a passionate and sexy all-encompassing kiss. My heightened feelings were obvious, since this was a first-time experience for me and Jason was upstairs and could have woken up and caught us at any moment. I didn't care. I wanted fun and attention and he wasn't giving it to me.

That very week, our escapades grew even more controversial when we were found kissing and fondling each other in the field by the pub. We were found by the local boys, who were about twenty years old, themselves and, not surprisingly, wanted to join in. I found myself in an orgy, getting attention from all directions and feeling incredibly alive, playing out this dangerous version of me. It's interesting to think about ourselves as different versions of ourselves. We all wear masks, wanting to make impressions or exude a certain image. We even play characters and roles in our lives, and this exploration of myself enabled me to test the boundaries of responsibility and limits. The question is: does the mask we wear serve us, and, furthermore, when is it time to release it? So many people have a permanent, unrealised mask, never truly opening themselves to the wider world or, even more disturbingly, to themselves.

Whilst I was becoming more promiscuous outside of work, I began to bring these antics to the workplace. Stuart, the assistant manager, was thirty years old and engaged to a chubby secretary who also worked in the town centre. According to him, he had a boring life and would soon be married to a boring woman until my promiscuous self turned up at work one day and enticed him with my wild ways. Flirting with him with no regard for consequence I began to flaunt myself at him, testing this new control mechanism I had discovered, getting attention my way whenever I wanted it. Boy, oh boy, did it work! He was hooked. Falsified trips to the storeroom above the shop started happening, with secret groping and taunting movements constantly alluring him to me.

I was in a position of power, and soon enough we were finding more opportunities to have sex in the middle of the day at work. He always smelled of smoke and had a slightly salty taste to his lips. Although I was slightly repelled, the danger allured me regardless. We took it too far one day when we decided that we had five minutes until closing time and his fiancé was on her way to pick him up. The shop and the street were peaceful and quiet, so we had sex on the counter in the shop, brazenly testing the danger boundary of being caught – anyone could walk through the door at any time. We were never caught. However, I quickly had enough of him and moved swiftly on to other targets on the main street, flirting and prancing around like I owned the place.

Jason decided to take a new job far away from Hampshire. We were still together, if you can call it being together, and I wasn't fazed. He was apathetic towards me, knowing full well what I was up to. He didn't once approach me about it. I found him spineless and didn't respect him much for his lack of action; it just fuelled my belief that I was right in taking charge of my own life and that he was suffering from his own lack of action. I created a belief for myself that encouraged me to be ruthless in my actions with others, as they certainly wouldn't stand up for or look out for me. Neither of us letting go, we agreed to have a long-distance relationship, which I never truly considered something I would do again. Internally, however, as far as I was concerned he was gone, and out of sight is out of mind.

Emma and I continued our rampaging with nothing in our way, having the time of our lives. I moved out of the house Jason and I shared and into a shared house in the town centre with people all in their twenties. I paid rent once again and was left with a measly nine pounds a week to buy food. I lived on frozen sausages and microwaved potatoes. It was all I needed and I felt free and in control again. Starting to go to clubs, meeting new and exciting people, drinking alcohol, and generally causing men to fall at their knees, I continued this lifestyle until one day everything I knew changed.

I suspect you've had this unconscious experience yourself, the experience that life or something seemingly outside of your awareness has made a decision, a decision you must know about and that you are compelled to see in your own reflection. Some call it having a mirror metaphorically held up to your face, where you are shown what you couldn't see before, perhaps a mirror that unveils a mask. One sunny day I was walking down the high street on my break after having visited a handsome French man who was old enough to be my father. I was at his shop for some quick flirting, kissing, and fondling when I quite unexpectedly saw Jason walking down the street. I was surprised, as in my mind he really was out of sight and out of mind. He jumped in front of me with a big smile and beamed, 'Surprise!' His face was lit up; he showed more physical expression than usual, pushing his hands out from his sides like people do when they announce themselves unexpectedly. I was so full of myself that I just kept walking, almost dismissive of him – I really couldn't be bothered. Perhaps it was the shock of knowing that I'd now have to deal with him and his expectations. Frankly, it felt to me that this sudden appearance was an inconvenience, so I blocked out his presence. Unsurprisingly, he started shouting at me, saying I was selfish and that he'd come all this way to surprise me and be with me and there I was being so horrible to him. I didn't even turn around or take another look. I just walked on as if he wasn't there. Out of sight, out of mind. He had finally shown that emotion I had longed for earlier, but it was too little, too late. He drove off angrily with his dog by his side.

The universal message showing me that I was becoming careless, heartless, and self-consumed continued to reveal itself one morning not long after my final encounter with Jason. I had asked one of my flatmates to help me fix my radiator, and he banged on my door very early to assist me. I had yet another man in my bed. This wasn't an unusual occurrence, as I had been experiencing many men and their desires for me. The flatmate came in, sorted out my radiator, and, as he left, said to another flatmate, 'She's got another one in there with her'. I actually felt mortified. It was like this flatmate was holding up another metaphorical mirror to my face and showing me a perception that hadn't been clear to me before. To others, I looked like a slut. I realised deep down in my own sense of self that this was how I felt and was actually allowing myself to feel: useable. I have nothing against people having sexual free rein based on their own free will, though I realised that mine wasn't a conscious, choice with free beliefs. These actions were unconscious cravings for external validation. These actions were not respectable or self-loving.

With this revelation, I turned away all men who came to my door, said goodbye to Emma, and called my dad. He and his friend Gordon came in two cars to pick me and my things up and I left that dangerous sexual world to go back to my family home at the age of seventeen to set myself straight – or so I thought.

A Flourishing Mind

'Experience is a hard teacher because she gives the test first, the lesson afterward.'

Vernon Law

Chapter 4
Rampage Returns

Seeing my dad again, and hearing him on the phone asking me if I wanted him to come and pick me up, was such a feeling of lightness and relief. He must have sensed in my tone that I was out of control and decided to give me the out I needed – a chance to reign myself in. He drove up to the house I was living in in Hampshire, a three-hour drive, with his friend in tow, ready to take me home. Seeing his smiling face in his car as he approached felt like home, and I realised how much I'd missed him. I felt dirty and used from my rampaging adventures exploring my boundaries. Even though I knew I'd created this situation myself, I wanted to once again be cared for, and perhaps this was my father's time to come back into my life to care for me. Driving back through the countryside to Kent, the trees and fields whizzing past me, I had time to be a child again under my father's protection. I was going home. We arrived and Sara was there to greet me. It seemed as if my father had softened somewhat over the time I had been gone. He was less aggressive and certainly more thoughtful in his approach towards me – perhaps Sara had a positive effect on him. I entered my familiar bedroom, the one I had grown up in, for the most part, and resumed my life much as it had been before I left – perhaps apart from my new-found experiences and knowledge of the world and, indeed, myself.

I had secretly called Carol, Suzanne's mother, to alert her to my return. I wanted to surprise Suzanne, as I'd missed her incredibly. Carol was thrilled to know I was retuning and disclosed to me that Suzanne would be beyond excited that I was to come home. Apparently she had missed me enormously and would be beside herself to have me back in her life, her soulmate by her side once again. Not a single day passed before I was on my way down the street, past the cobbled red brick wall, making my way a few doors down to Suzanne's family home. Walking in quietly, knowing that Carol was expecting me, Suzanne was covertly directed to the kitchen table whilst I snuck around the house, ready to do my best 'surprise' impression. As I approached the door, I realised I was very different now and had a moment of reflection, even though it was very fleeting, realising that we could be very different from one another, much as Jason and I were now, that maybe we wouldn't be best friends, we wouldn't be soulmates anymore. I pushed these thoughts aside and focused on the present moment and the task at hand: surprising my best friend.

I walked quietly through the door and saw Carol smiling to herself whilst Suzanne slouched at the table nibbling on a snack, talking to the others in the room. I announced myself with humbleness and slight hesitation, as if I were stepping back into another familiar world, hoping to be accepted back into the fold. Well, Suzanne's face was a scene in itself: she leaped up out of her chair, all food and talking disregarded, and literally flung herself at me, body, mind, and soul. The twenty-year-old version of her was much the same as when I left for my mother's a few years ago. Her new boyfriend Julian was in on the surprise, but I'd never met him before today, only heard about him. Seeing her again and knowing nothing had changed eased my mind and I felt increasingly happy to be home.

Settling back into my old life was relatively easy. The restrictions and expectations I had before from my father were gone. He was far more respectful of my individuality and independence. I suppose in some way, though I'll never know for sure, he instinctively knew I'd had a hard road and wanted to provide some comfort. His relationship with Sara seemed to be going well on the surface, until one day I returned home to find her crying at the front door, her car packed and saying a heartfelt goodbye to my father. It was a summer's day, creating a slight hazy effect with a feeling of damp closeness in the air. Sara was dressed in a pretty dress, with her car filled to the brim with her possessions. She would have been in her mid-twenties at this point and I could only assume ready to live and be free. Once again my father's impact on his loved ones made them feel trapped. In her case, although none of it was intentional, having been a teenager when she met him and subsequently married him, she had lost part of her growing up period and was ready to fly the nest and find her independence. I sensed this difficult moment for both of them in the driveway, my father being sensitive and careful, treating her delicately. Afterwards he expressed to me a wise inherent understanding that this day had to come. Sara felt terrible about leaving but was being pulled towards living her life with people her own age rather than settling with a man in his mid-fifties. Wanting to leave them to their moment, I said a hasty but meaningful goodbye to Sara and disappeared inside.

My father's adventure with Sara was essentially over, and it left him alone at a point in his life where he had given up his international driving career, had two heart attacks, said goodbye to his love, and found me, his daughter, back in his life. My father had another daughter from his first marriage. Her name is Jacqui, though apart from a very fleeting moment when I was around five years old, she'd never been in his life and I'd only ever met her once. My cousin Lisa, who was born of my father's sister, is eight years older than me. Apart from her on my father's side, no other family existed. Just us.

Being back in Kent, I applied for jobs and found a quick and easy one in the town centre of Ashford looking after a small bedding and soft furnishing store. As the only employee of the store, my responsibility was to order in new stock, arrange it in the shop, and sell it. Simple! My sole purpose at this point was to earn enough money to contribute a little to the household kitty and get money to have fun going out with friends. Suzanne and Julian made a great couple, and by spending more and more time with them, we all became fast friends. Julian kindly accepted that I was a major part of his girlfriend's world and I became the third wheel, once again under the protection and support of my dearest friend.

My education plans went by the wayside, and having achieved only average scores on my GCSEs – high school grades – I didn't have any aspirations for learning or for my future education. I just wanted to have fun. All my school friends were focused on their chosen studies or career paths, namely becoming dentist's assistants, as that was all that was really available for them at the time in our town. I wonder what their parents must have thought of me, especially as I was considered by many at one time to be the 'one' who would make it and succeed most in our friendship group. Society has its way of expecting us to behave, to succeed in certain ways, and there was an underlying although not easy to articulate feeling that I wasn't living to the potential that others preciously deemed or believed I had inside myself.

Bringing with me my new-found sexual appetite, my experiences, and my universal reflections, the pace of life slowed down a bit, perhaps, though not completely. My ability to continue to attract men at a rate of knots continued, and whilst making the rounds at the town pubs and clubs after work and on weekends – as a nearly adult female who had been away and returned – I was proving to be a great draw-card. A lot of what occurred in the nightlife of our small town for our age group was driving around town in hotted up cars with noisy exhausts and loud music blaring. When we weren't in clubs, Suzanne and our group of friends tended to join this convoy of cars making laps around the town centre. We were meeting up and swapping music, having a drink for the non-drivers, and generally kissing boys, flirting, and having fun with less danger and risk than I'd experienced before. This was relatively tame compared to my escapades with Emma. These were people I'd known all my life, and there was history, and with history there isn't much anonymity. Being back with these people felt safe, and I behaved a little more respectfully.

That year, Suzanne and Julian grew apart. He wasn't as daring or vivacious as perhaps she needed in a boyfriend, and we found ourselves footloose and fancy free, roaming the streets of our town looking for excitement. As we went to more places where alcohol was served, I found the old me from Hampshire resuming, and once again my life began to spin out of control. I started binge drinking heavily and, frankly, looking for sex to fulfil a false sense of security, security that I had rarely had in my life. Living at my family home meant that I wasn't able to go home with my lovers and had to find new and creative ways to be intimate with them outdoors, in other people's houses, and at parties. I was still working during the day, and you could call partying my other full-time job; it was starting to take its toll on my wellbeing.

By this time I was seventeen. I was functioning enough to get by, but I was on the verge of exhaustion, as I just wasn't limiting my exuberance. My father witnessed this craziness happening before his eyes. He was often the one to drop me off in town at night, and he gave me extra money to have fun with. Naturally, it was easy for him to see that I was spiralling out of control. He decided to give me a curfew. Funny, isn't it? I'd been homeless, fended for myself for a couple of years alone with no parents, and now, close to coming of age, I was on curfew. The rules were that I had to be home by midnight on workdays. When he told me, I breathed a sigh of relief. I needed someone to take control, someone to tell me this is how it must be to look after myself. When the rule was set, I thanked my dad and told him, 'I needed that'.

On one particular night I was with a man about six years older than I was. I'd known him most of my teenage life, as his brother went to my school. He was known for being dangerous despite being a social worker and having a caring side. His polarity in behaviour showed that he liked to test the boundaries. As you know, polarities exist in many places in life. Think about day and night, dark and light, happy and sad. We, and all that surround us, are a polarity. This guy loved to take his experiences to the end of every possible scale.

We were in his room at his house. There were Smashing Pumpkins band posters all over his walls, and heavy music was playing loudly. He was getting close to very drunk and soon began to get quite rough with me. Passionate sex was one thing, but ripping my knickers off and holding me down was another. He was getting out of control, and I was scared. Having to be back home by midnight, I had to somehow get out of his grip and convince him to walk me home. I didn't want to be there with him anymore. I was feeling incredibly unsafe. Living in a village just outside the main town meant my walks home were in dark places where woods teetered on the outskirts and shadows lurked. I needed him to keep me safe and walk me home. Eventually, with my knickers torn and sex aborted, he reluctantly agreed to walk with me. It was getting close to midnight and I knew that the wrath of my father's rules, even when conveniently agreed to by me, weren't worth being late home.

As we began walking in the still darkness, being drunk and having not gotten his way, he continued to hound me with sexual advances. His arm flung around my shoulders, pushing me into hedges that would hide us on the main road. I pushed him heavily away once more. At this point his temper snapped. He called me a tease and a bitch, he shouted that he didn't know why he bothered with me, and he left me in the darkness, alone. Walking home, I was cold and trembling, jumping at every turn, worried that I was about to be attacked. Getting home seemed to take an eternity, and a feeling of relief once again washed over me when I arrived. We never saw each other again. Whilst it may seem enough for me to learn some lessons about my safety and self-worth, it seemed I needed one more lesson in the same vein before I truly understood the danger I was putting myself in with my promiscuous behaviour.

I don't even know his name. All I know is that he was a man, a beautiful man who I met at a nightclub. I'd had my eagle eye on him all night whilst completely and utterly setting myself a challenge that he would want me too. He was very different from all my other conquests, as he was sophisticated, upper-class, and very well-dressed in a white shirt and well-tailored suit; he had short, jet-black hair, fair eyes, and a sexy, aloof attitude to boot. I'd heard he was a male model. I practically threw myself at him, being blocked by him at every turn like he was swatting a fly away. His friends were amused by me and willing to bat me around like a cat would a mouse whilst going in for the kill. Well, I had persistence like a cat and kept my own prey in sight until eventually, after a few hours, more drinks, and a drunk male model, I won the battle of wills. He agreed to be intimate with me.

Taking him back to my friend's house like I'd won a prize, along with his friends and mine, we made our way back to the spare room. I was in heaven because he wanted me, which meant in my mind that I was worthwhile. Those sexy men looked so out of place there in that humble home of humble people. Like a rock band waiting in an airport with the everyday people milling around, they stood out. Upstairs, as we began to take our clothes off, his apathetic hesitation still in play, I started to realise what I was doing. I was about to have sex with a stranger who didn't really want to have sex with me; I was his only option this late at night. As we began to have sex, I realised I didn't want to. Let's pause here. This becomes a controversial point; the legal term is 'date rape'. The contentious issue is that I obviously, undoubtedly led him on. Even I am not sure I truly know how to feel about this situation. So many people are date raped and raped, and the question of mixed messages come up, particularly in my situation. In the end, I believe 'forcing' anyone to do anything is not acceptable.

I pushed him away whilst he was in full motion inside of me. I said no and that I didn't want to continue:

'Please stop!' I said. It was like his drunken mind couldn't hear me: we were going all the way and I had no choice. No. No. No. Stop. He didn't. After a little longer and a bit of a panicked struggle, he stopped before he ejaculated and became like a dead weight on top of me. He was a heaving mass that suddenly didn't seem quite as beautiful as before. He was asleep – I couldn't make up my mind, was he Beauty or the Beast? I ran downstairs to my friends, telling them he wouldn't stop. They looked at me with little surprise and not much care. At that point I realised I had been asking for his attention all night, practically throwing myself at him, and had gotten what I asked for. I had just changed my mind at the wildest moment. His friends woke him up and took him away, never to be seen in our town again. I learned a lot about beauty that night, learned never to judge a book by its cover. This final lesson learned, my life started to change once again, this time on a slight upward trend.

Eastwell Manor is an expansive mansion built in 1022, where King Edward and Queen Victoria are said to have stayed during their respective reigns. This wondrous historic place was only one mile from my house and was well known as a place famous people and royalty from Europe stayed. With only twenty-one rooms in the manor, sprawling ballrooms and fine dining areas abound. Entering the building was like walking back in time. Wanting to be paid well, and having left my soft furnishings job, I applied for a position as a housekeeper at Eastwell Manor – which was something I thought I could do. Upon being accepted on a shift rotation, I joined the back of house staff to service the rich and well-to-do. I donned a spectacular uniform consisting of a long, black, flowing dress nipped at my waist with the sleeves puffed and frilled at the seams where my shoulders were. The dress ran to the ankle, with buttons fastening the fabric at the front. A white apron was placed over the top that when positioned covered the front of the dress and crossed over at the back in a crisscross fashion, much as in the olden days in which the building belonged.

Working at the manor brought me a new sense of freedom. As I had once again fallen into the trap of flaunting myself and being self-destructive, this job and place gradually influenced me positively. Its rural and royal surroundings were easy to feel admiration in, as if the physical walls and romantic history infused my skin. It was easy to feel respect working there. As the grounds were vast, separate staff quarters lay within the acreage where many of the staff lived. Ironically, these were the grounds Jason had worked at when I first met him at the fish and chip shop of course, he was far away from the place now. Due to its fine attributes, people were attracted from around the UK and Europe to train and work there as waiters and waitresses, chefs, and front of house staff. Because of the long hours of hospitality and the remoteness of the location, the living area was a blessing for those who worked a long way from home. Naturally, with people who were generally at a young age living in close proximity to each other and with very little personal space, all sorts of varied friendships were born.

I worked with a team of eight other women and one man, and we became close, sharing our thoughts of the world whilst we worked. It was hard and demanding work, cleaning twenty-one rooms that were each the size of today's modern houses and conceivably even bigger. Cleaning the rooms required four people in one room at any given time. We worked well as a team, and consequently I began to make new friends who knew nothing of my past or my story, and I slowly integrated my familiar childhood friends with fresh new friendships with my new workmates. Still a young seventeen, I loved this new life, where my job was unusual and brought me new experiences that included history and helping guests have a magical stay. Whilst Suzanne was still very much in my life, the other people I'd met, who were essentially her friends, dropped away. I'm not going to pretend that my time at Eastwell Manor didn't include having fun, going to parties, and generally flirting with boys – in fact, I had a few short-term relationships, an upgrade if you will from the one-night stands, progressing to weeks rather than nights, like I had fleetingly experienced before – but the very essence of this place had an old presumed safety within it, and the people around me were much like siblings, looking out for each other. The management were almost akin to the parent role, ensuring we stayed under control.

As I only lived a mile away, I walked to and from work every day. The walk in the crisp country air did me good. I had time to think and reflect by myself. Living at home became easy; my curfew lifted and a sense of normalcy arose. It was at this time, whilst I was with a guy called Simon, one of the junior chefs, that I became quite ill. One night whilst staying over at his room in the staff quarters, we were both sound asleep in the middle of the night. I began to shake uncontrollably and had an incredibly high fever; I was cold to the touch and sweating terribly. Persevering through the night and making it to work in the morning, I felt very ill. Simon was worried about me and alerted my teammates to look after me during the day. Donna, another chambermaid, and I were cleaning a massive marble bath together – a two-person job – and whilst cleaning I became very faint and couldn't stand. My father was called, as was an ambulance, and I was taken to the very hospital I was born in. My father met me there and wheeled me around to the emergency area. Thinking he was being funny, he did wheelies with the wheelchair, tipping and spinning and making me even dizzier, using his humour to try to mask his fear.

After immediate tests, it was confirmed that I had contracted Staphylococcus aureus bacteraemi. This is an infection that can be picked up anywhere and lives on the skin; if it enters the blood system, it can become life-threatening. In a nutshell, I had blood poisoning. When further tests were performed, it also became clear that the infection was in my Gynaecological area and that I needed to be treated immediately. After some basic surgery, I lay waiting for the doctor to come and give me the test results. Perhaps I should have realised at the time that the news was bad, as a nurse was on guard with me and didn't leave my side, patiently waiting for the doctor to arrive.

Lying in a hospital bed in the recovery area with the standard green curtain shielding me from view, the doctor appeared and delivered the news. The nurse dutifully held my hand, soothing me and hushing me as I lay in the bed being told that I would never be able to have children. The doctor informed me that I had this infection and that he had also uncovered another disease that would affect my life in many ways yet to come: endometriosis. As I lay there with the nurse holding my hand, my father hurriedly arrived at my side, nervous to hear the news. The nurse relayed what the doctor said, as I was upset and still processing and taking in the news.

My father's reaction was classic Dad. Upon hearing the news, he said, 'Oh, is that all? I thought you had cancer or something'. It was a relief to him, pain for me, although I understand his whimsical and thoughtless sentiment now even though it hurt at the time. My mother had been riddled with cancer when I was born, and he had already spent a lot of time in hospitals with her over the years. Still, at the present time, lying in the hospital bed, all I had for comfort was this nurse, a stranger to me. It's not that I ever thought about having children at this stage in my life; I just knew I'd lost something I'd never have the chance to experience. It wasn't long before I was back at work, where worried co-workers were relieved I was back and on the mend. This part of the story will develop later.

As the months moved on, so did Simon. We were really only a short-term duo. He wanted to be together more often, wanted more of an emotional connection from me, though I'd lost interest. I suspect you are starting to see the pattern here: me being in complete control of my relationships, me initiating them, controlling them, and destroying them before they destroyed me. Knowing what I know now as a qualified human behaviour professional, it's obvious that I was rarely safe as a child, that I was exploited and exposed to very high levels of stress and insecurity. It's no wonder I craved attention and a sense of safety in whatever form I could conjure it. Even though my relationships were short, I was becoming more of an adult and understanding that not everything revolved around me. I was making more new groups of friends and in particular was having fun with the chefs in the kitchen. One guy in particular used to make funny noises and call out as we walked past to the tea break room on our breaks. I loved to laugh and join in.

One evening, a group of us decided to go to the Ministry of Sound in a town an hour or so away. Those of you who know the Ministry of Sound know it was a brilliant gig in the 1990s, and it was so amazing to be able to go. I met Phil, the junior sous chef, in his room as planned, and low and behold no-one else turned up. Phil and I, not knowing each other all that well, decided to go with the flow and let the evening evolve naturally. I had a little money saved and could pay for both of us for the night. We set out on our merry way to Maidstone, the town where we would change transport to get to the gig.

After arriving in Maidstone and drawing money from the ATM – a hole in the wall – it became apparent that I didn't have any money. I had miscalculated the sums, leaving us with a grand total of five pounds for the entire evening's entertainment, including getting back to the manor. Phil had already told me he'd spent all his pay, so couldn't withdraw anything either. Being thoroughly wise, we bought two drinks at the nearest bar with the coins in our pockets and drank them down determinedly. Catching the train back for 'free' to the nearest station to the manor, we were still a good one and a half hours walk away from the manor. Approaching the nearest taxi, we explained that we had only this single five-pound note and asked him if he would drive us to the manor. He graciously accepted, and we were saved!

As we arrived back at the staff quarters, people were in full party mode, with the drinks flowing and music pumping, so Phil and I joined in. Dancing, laughing, and getting on so well, the night ended with a kiss. I knew I wasn't going to have sex with this guy just yet: we'd connected on a different level than I had connected with a man before. There was respect and no expectation about what was to happen, just connection. It's amazing that I am writing about my husband of eighteen years. In fact, the day I started this book was the day we had our seventeenth anniversary of the night I just described. From November 2, 1996, we were hooked on each other, and nothing has been able to tear us apart since. Becoming a real couple and doing lots of activities, touristy drives, pub crawls, and staff parties, we had a blast getting to know each other more deeply than just an animal attraction. We were exploring each other's intellects, dreams, and hopes. He was twenty-six and I was seventeen, and we adored getting to know each other in many different ways. Suzanne met Phil and loved him too. Although she was not as much a part of the picture as she had been for the first fifteen years of my life, Suzanne was always there in the background. She was happy and had moved in with a new boyfriend of her own.

Meeting my father was always interesting for my boyfriends, as my father enjoyed intimidating and patronising people to see how and when they would crack. This didn't happen so much with Phil. He had a quiet assurance about him – nothing to prove, just him. Not to mention he was bigger than my dad! Phil had recently come back from Australia on a yearlong working holiday where his then girlfriend broke their relationship apart, and he had returned a single man. Having been a worldly traveller when exploring different countries in the truck, we had that adventurer's spirit in common. A few couples formed that year at the manor, and we often hung out together, creating our own little group of people in love. Roughly six months after we met, Phil received a surprise phone call from Melbourne, Australia, asking him if he'd be interested in coming back as a sponsored resident for one of the city's most revered restaurants at the time – Le Restaurant, Sofitel. Having loved his time in Australia, this appealed to Phil, and he asked if I wanted to come along. Being the spontaneous crazy person I am, not afraid to discover, I immediately said yes. And so it was that we were going to Melbourne, Australia – but not before a few hurdles, naturally.

'Progress is impossible without change, and those who cannot change their minds cannot change anything.'

George Bernard Shaw

Chapter 5
The Wonderful World of Aus

Being seventeen years old when you need to be eighteen to get a working holiday visa to Australia is a somewhat annoying problem. My friend Suzanne was absolutely adamant that I was never really going to go, and my parents didn't seem fazed either way, though they were happy to go with whatever I decided. Naturally, this made me even more determined to do what I wanted. Phil planned his move to Melbourne in May 1997. I turned eighteen in April, just before Phil left, and he arranged a beautiful surprise with a once in a lifetime opportunity to dine and stay where we both worked at the exclusive Eastwell Manor. Our friends and colleagues rallied around us to ensure we had an amazing time, with waiters smiling their brightest smiles, photos taken of my momentous occasion – I felt incredibly special.

Just thinking about being apart from Phil for two months filled my heart with dread. Meeting Phil's mother Rosalie and his sister Anne for the first time on the night he departed for Australia was a fantastic surprise. Originally from the spectacular city of Bath, the two ladies drove all the way to Kent to pick Phil and I up and take us to London Heathrow. My emotions were running high and I was beside myself, crying. I clung to Phil and did not want to let him go. Rosalie was kind and smiling. In the car when we were returning to Kent, having said goodbye to her son, my lover, my heart hurting and a heavy weight upon me, she said, 'It's alright, my love, he's not gone forever. You'll see him again soon'. Her words soothed me for a while until I fell asleep in the back of the car for the rest of the journey home. As I was dropped at my doorstep, I left the car with little in the way of thanks or goodbye to Phil's family and went inside. I didn't realise at the time that they had travelled a special five-hour round trip to drop me off before going back home again. This is just another example of being completely within my own world, focusing on my own circumstances and not yet having the capacity to see beyond my own perspective.

Phil settled happily into life at the hotel in Melbourne. As I was yet to arrive and planned to do so in the next two months once my visa arrived, he was treated to living in a room at the hotel as his staff quarters. It was all part of the relocation package offered to international staff. We wrote letters often. There weren't yet mobile phones and we were only just getting the gist of old-fashioned coding on the new computers that were in our homes, schools, or workplaces. Access to the Internet had barely arrived in my hometown. We made expensive phone calls to each other frequently:

lovers confessing they missed each other and couldn't possibly wait until June, when I would finally arrive in Australia.

Meanwhile in the UK, I was impatient, desperately missing Phil. I would sometimes sit by the phone just waiting and watching it until it rang. It was like my heart was perpetually in my mouth. Anticipation. With my aeroplane ticket bought and my visa stamped, I just waited for the date to roll around, lingering until my visa said I could enter Australia – it was pure agony. There is nothing I regret in my life, as I believe all actions are learning, though the next part of my story is something I feel remorse about – not for my lessons, as I certainly learned some big lessons here, but for the pain I caused because of my actions.

Missing Phil, I was once again on my own, and Suzanne was preparing to be apart from me once more, even though she still didn't think I would actually leave! Whilst waiting for my departure date, we resumed our old routine of being together and finding fun parties to attend. I saw old friends whilst continuing my new friendships at the Manor and set out to drown my sorrows and get attention once again. New bars were popping up in town and we found more places to venture out to. My co-worker Jon, who was the only male chambermaid, knew Phil too and was my connection and confidant for my feelings during this temporary separation. Jon was a very tall, lanky man in his mid-twenties. His dark, drooping eyes looked permanently sad, even on the verge of apathy, but they were deep and mysterious. I suspect it was because he was stoned most of the time. When he walked, he lurched forward with his back stooped. He was slow and methodical, philosophical and kind. His dad was the town driving instructor, so we often zoomed around in the learner's car, looking like a bunch of cool kids in a dorky kind of a way.

Jon and I went out one night to see the band he was playing in. Suzanne accompanied me to have some fun before I left for my Australian adventure. At the bar, it was small and colourful, with lots of haze immersing the room. The atmosphere was sultry. We were playing a drinking game with the Greek drink Sambuca and the shots were literally set alight and flaming. I was winning, and with every win, a free shot of alcohol was awarded. I was blazingly sloshed and loving being the centre of attention. The music was amazing: lots of sexy beats, slow and emotional. I met Will. Will was one of my chambermaid co-workers' brothers, and Jon's best friend. I knew his family mostly from school, though he and his sister were a lot older than me. There was something about him that reminded me of Kurt Cobain. I felt that old feeling in the pit of my stomach, my old friend and foe: danger. The flirting continued as the night went on. Will was somewhat of a hermit, and his mates were egging him on. My competitive spirit of winning the man returned anew, and the game was on. We kissed at the bar and in the car on the way back to his house. These kisses turned into a frenzied sexual encounter at his house, with his parents in the very next room.

I had done something terrible. I had cheated on Phil, the very man I was pining for. The week before this event, I had undergone my first operation for the endometriosis. The operation aimed to alleviate my pain levels, and I know that after the operation I was feeling vulnerable. I am aware that this doesn't excuse my behaviour. I was feeling the old trap once more, that feeling of being out of control, of hurting and needing comfort. My friend Vicki, who was a childhood friend, was also with this crowd, and she knew of my emotional and physical pain. She tried to encourage me to stay in England, as did Will's sister. They wanted me to be a part of their lives. I didn't want to be. I knew I had done wrong. I became increasingly evasive on the phone with Phil and couldn't be as adoring or loving as I used to. I was cutting off and disconnecting from my emotions. I didn't want to hurt over what I'd done. I didn't want to face the darker side of myself. I could feel myself playing the other old manipulative game, pushing him away and being destructive. To face my demons, I faced up to my actions and changed the historical trends by deciding to go all the way to Australia to tell Phil in person what I'd done.

The time came to leave England. It was time to leave my friends and begin my adventure of flying across the world to a land I knew nothing about – well, save for *Home and Away* on the TV. I'd never even been on an aeroplane before! It was fine, though; I had travelled the world, hadn't I? I had been to many countries in Europe and could easily get myself around. Gathered at the airport waiting to enter into customs, you could cut the tension in the air with a knife. My mother, Frank, and my father were all in the same space for the first time in almost eight years. They sat opposite each other like opponents at a boxing match ready for their match to begin, sizing each other up with glaring eyes.

Unsurprisingly, I was feeling unsettled, as I'd only just said goodbye to all my friends at a party the night before. I'd packed my only suitcase full of clothes and CDs and here everyone was, about to send me on my way. Crying, feeling somewhat sad and lonesome, I said goodbye to each parent. I walked to the departure gate, where once through the other side of the doors, I would be out of sight. I paused. As I gave my tickets to the airline staff member, I walked through the barrier door and stopped. I turned around with red eyes and tears on my face. Looking back at my disjointed family, I waved. They waved back with sadness and worry in their eyes, something I had rarely seen before. This sight crept inside of me and turned into a feeling, an emotion that expressed a new realisation. It was a realisation that indicated to me that perhaps I was loved by them in their way. Turning, I vanished around the corner into the departure terminal. Alone. I just kept breathing, feeling the air inside my lungs, searching for some way to create regularity. Big fat tears threatened to spill over onto my cheeks.

Once I'd made it around the corner, the bright lights of the terminal welcomed me and I felt more buoyant instantly – I was going to Australia! With hours to wait before boarding the aeroplane, I called people from the telephone box with my loose change. I chatted until the money ran dry. Boarding my plane, I was in the smoking section, which didn't bother me at first as I smoked quite a bit myself; that said, halfway through the flight I wanted to get off because the smoke was totally consuming and suffocating! I was seated in the back of the Greek aeroplane next to some cheerful Kentish people going to Melbourne as well. They became my companions across the vast world in which we were travellers. Stopping in Athens and then Bangkok, the flight to Melbourne took an agonising twenty-four hours. During the time on the plane I had fizzy drink spilt on my jeans by the flight attendant during a period of turbulence. Fizzy drinks are a sticky substance, which is quite unconfortable in long-distance travel. I took off one boot and then realised I couldn't get it back on due to swollen feet, so I began a lopsided walk through Bangkok airport with one shoe on and one shoe off. Finally, there was a tragic experience where a fellow passenger quite near to us died as we were landing in Melbourne. The flight attendants shouted at me in Greek, trying to express some instructions I couldn't comprehend. Even though I had had many experiences in my life, these were all new and certainly adventurous ones!

Arriving in Melbourne was exciting. It was exciting to hear the Australian accent for the first time and to see buildings throughout the airport that were very different from London's. Phil was waiting expectantly for me in the arrivals area, and internally I was churning at the thought of seeing him. I was here now, but what the hell was I doing? I quickly became aware that I was the type to follow things through, but not necessarily the type to think things through. Our reunion was strange and stilted. Phil seemed confused, perhaps because I was resistant. We held hands in the taxi back to the new unit he had secured for us, but I was acting strangely and he had no idea why.

Once we were back at the unit, we decided to see a bit of Melbourne. I was tired but needed air, and we walked Chapel St in Toorak looking for a place to eat. Phil, being a very intuitive person, gently kept asking what was wrong. Whilst eating lunch I explained to him that I'd slept with someone else. Not only did I explain this to him, but I delivered the message without emotion or care. In fact, I delivered it with pride. It was pride of my honesty, honesty I'd rarely been shown in my life. His reaction was awful; he was sick to his stomach and couldn't believe what was happening. I started to see the effect I was having and began to feel some emotion. I wanted to comfort him. I was being unintentionally manipulative, playing with his feelings. Over the next few days, things gradually turned around. We worked through the hurt and I knew I had to build his trust in me back up, which took a long time. The universe was obviously sending me this gift of a human being, as his patience, kindness, and perseverance paid off. In fact, these moments, and his ability to help me even when he was hurting, happened more than just this once in my life.

Living in Melbourne was a shock to my system. Phil was working longer hours than I was used to in England. I was left to find my own way around a new city where I couldn't work out how to use basic amenities like pay phones or ATMs because they were so vastly different from the ones I knew. It felt like a fog had come over me. I knew no-one, had little interaction with anyone, and the city was so vast and spread out I couldn't make head or tail of the place. More loneliness enveloped me. I needed to find work and looked through the papers, not truly understanding where the locations were or how to get to them even if I did get an interview.

Phil was a bit more experienced at this, being older than me and having lived in Australia for a year prior. Unfortunately, he often wasn't around and I couldn't always get access to his help. I was finally interviewed for a job a few weeks after arriving at a very up-market pharmacy in a very expensive part of Toorak. I got a job as a 'cash and wrap girl'. I'd never heard this terminology before – it seemed so foreign! Receiving my uniform, I started taking orders from the customers and helping them pay. This was a very different experience to the fish and chip shop serving skill. Here, politeness and, to be quite honest, being stuck-up was a virtue. I didn't gel well and made a few people cringe with my frankness and boldness.

Through this job, I met the most wonderful woman, Robyn. In her late forties, a Kiwi from New Zealand with bold red hair and blue mascara on her eyelashes, she was a mother hen. Seeing that I was a little lost and going beyond herself, she took me under her wing and showed me the ropes. She stood up for me against the managers when they insisted I wear make-up when I really didn't want to. Robyn was a lady who knew her own mind and wasn't afraid to speak up. She became someone I loved, as did her entire family. My life is truly enriched simply for knowing her. Her husband John was a sales expert, taking the world by storm in the field of sales. Leah and Sacha, her two beautiful daughters, were incredibly accepting of me and treated me like a sister, with grace.

Whilst my adult life officially started here, my confusion and increasing anger towards the world did too. On the outside I appeared a capable, together and friendly girl, but this kind of normal didn't feel accessible to me; it was something I couldn't quite grasp. I didn't belong in this world. I felt like when there wasn't a fight, drama, or terrible occurrence happening in my life, I didn't understand what life was for. These thoughts were not entirely conscious at the time, though in hindsight I can see so clearly that I was struggling to find meaning, struggling to understand what life was about, to understand what I was about. All I had was emotion without meaning, so I heightened those emotions and they just got bigger and bigger until they were ready to explode.

I made a few friends who didn't judge me or overexcite me. I went through a few jobs that began and ended as casual affairs. Phil continued to work at the Sofitel, evolving into an accomplished and professional chef. We had moved from the lovely unit in Toorak to a smaller, more affordable one in Richmond, not too far on the other side of the city. We had been getting on well, though my moods were plummeting often and I wasn't a young party girl anymore. I was now faithful and loving but felt increasingly depressed and sad. Phil still worked long hours. I continued to feel alone, save for Robyn, who would pick me up in her car. She would take me shopping and to cafes, encouraging me to interact with the world. I would often go to her house and have dinner, where I would be looked after and cuddled, listened to and included.

Phil's mum and sister came over for a trip around Australia and to visit us in the second year of our stay. I looked forward to going on holiday with them on a trip to the Great Ocean Road, a famous and stunning drive along the coast in Victoria. Phil took some time off and we set off on our adventure. Whilst I learned diplomacy at a young age, I had perhaps forgotten how to apply it and created awkward, jealous situations on otherwise lovely occasions. In my eyes, Phil gave his family the attention I craved, and although he was absolutely still in love with me, I started to act like a child. It's a way of acting I'd not experienced in myself before. I couldn't understand how to behave or belong in this scenario. Rosalie, Phil's mum, wasn't impressed and spent time chatting to her son about his unruly and often very rude girlfriend. I wasn't getting along well with his family, though they were trying hard.

My mother also decided to visit. She had left Frank, claiming that he was gay and had left her for an Asian transsexual. Who knows if this is true? Was it another lie? I didn't dare waste my time speculating and thinking about it. Phil still didn't quite get why my mum was difficult to be around. She played him well and he didn't see the conniving side I did, until one day she blatantly lied about something he had done directly to another person right in his presence and he had that awkward experience himself. He also began to see her true colours after experiencing her insatiable need to go on and on about the tiniest things until you thought your ears would bleed. She always had a hidden agenda and would exploit it as much as humanly possible. It wasn't the worst visit I've had with her. She was on her own, and we went to Sydney on a train and enjoyed ourselves as tourists. There was no-one else to compete with when it was just us and all those jealousies disappeared for that week. It was quite refreshing, and we really did have some fun.

During my mother's visit, she wanted me to see a doctor, as my mood swings were apparent. Upon visiting the GP, I reacted angrily when my mother made exaggerated claims about my moods. I was so tired with her after being together for only a few weeks that I raised my voice at her, which only encouraged the doctor to prescribe me anti-depressants. I'd been in the doctor's room for twenty minutes and walked out with a drug that only made my situation worse. Phil has a better recollection of this time than I do. According to him, I became flat and lifeless. I would swear that I was feeling better than ever, though he could see that I had lost my inner flair and that the drugs were taking away my emotion. I didn't feel, I didn't react, and I was lacking exuberance.

I put on a lot of weight and generally stopped caring about things, but inside I felt good. I felt stable and steady, though I didn't realise that I'd ceased to live deeply. Casual jobs still came and went. I did well at them but never really lasted, leaving before anything got too hard or required too much effort. Once again, I was skirting responsibilities and taking the easy road. I had learned this from my father. I still wasn't satisfied. Phil would come home at night and I'd be drinking a bottle of wine in the dark listening to Tracy Chapman, literally drowning my sorrows.

The time came when he decided that he'd had enough of my troublesome shenanigans. After three years of being together, he couldn't take it anymore and told me it was over. We agreed that I spend a few days at Robyn's house, and Leah, her daughter, took me out to see a band, but still I mostly cried all night long. A few unbearable days went by and I returned to our unit in Richmond to plead my case to Phil. I could absolutely see why he didn't want to be around me, and I wholeheartedly promised I would change. I would be a better person; I would stop the drama and get on with life, live to the fullest and experience it with him, presently and wholly. There's nothing like nearly losing something to kick you in the arse and scare the life into you, is there? I'm pleased to say I kept my promise, I did change, and I did (do) grow, learn, love and live more fully.

Phil agreed to give me another chance. We decided to hightail it out of Melbourne. After all, we hadn't gone all the way to Australia to be stuck in one place! I weaned myself off of my anti-depressants, which was a harrowing and nauseous experience. We planned to find a new home, to get away from the life we were trapping ourselves in.

The spontaneous girl in me came out and suggested that we get a map of Australia – I would close my eyes, swing around and point, and then we would go to the nearest major city to where my finger landed. So with excitement in the air and possibility enticing us, I swung around with my arm pointing outward and landed it on the map. It landed right near Perth. Perth! We quit our jobs, sold our furniture, and ended our lease, and within three weeks we had packed our car and trailer. We were ready to drive across the land, across the Nullarbor. Three days of driving and adventure were upon us, and I felt alive. We had no more than five hundred dollars to our names and knew that when we arrived in Perth we needed to find accommodation rapidly, with furniture included. We also needed to find jobs quickly to ensure that we had ongoing income. This all seemed a million years away as we journeyed across the vast desert.

On a Friday in late August 1999, we arrived and headed straight to Scarborough, right by the sea. Friends had told us it was a good place to start. Upon our arrival, we met a real estate agent who took us to Maylands, where we were to find a dingy little one-room ground floor unit that cost ninety dollars a week and was fully furnished, with about eighteen other identical units stacked around it. It was pokey and not particularly pleasant, but it was a place we could settle for now, a base that was ours. We unpacked the car late in the evening, tired from the thousands of kilometres we had driven. I fell asleep on the bed and in the morning awoke to kookaburra birds chanting their songs, their calls sounding like monkeys in the trees rather than birds. During the night Phil had completely set our unit up, and everything to do with moving in was done. I had slept through the entire night!

I walked straight into work – in fact, straight into a job that gave me a professional career and led me to where I am today. Phil found it harder to find meaningful work in Perth, as his skills outweighed the demand for fine dining, and he ended up working casually with an agency, filling in for people on leave and covering busy seasons. I made friends easily and met a lovely girl named Irene where I worked in East Perth, only minutes from where we lived. We were fast friends; she was two years older than me with Puerto Rican heritage and a curious and nomadic nature, which was different and fun. I began to wake up and live my life, choosing more frequently to be good, do well, and keep my promise to Phil to be better. At this stage in my life, being twenty years old and having been through so much already, I felt like some of my demons were at bay. Throughout the next few years, however they liked to surface every now and again, as you will find out.

We explored Perth and moved to a few different houses throughout the millennium year, and the early 2000s were good to us. Phil became an executive chef for the horseracing contingent and delved into his new management position with gusto. I continued to work at B Digital, a new and fast-growing company that sold mobile phones in a unique and simple way. I developed a passion for coaching people in the early years and quickly became a team leader of customer care teams. My decision-making skills and confident manner made people believe I could do a good job and build trust with others.

This had never happened to me before –being professionally believed in and considered worthwhile. Like my intimate relationships, my jobs had been a means to an end, not a worthwhile pursuit that was to be worked hard for. I suddenly found myself in a stable relationship and with a stable job, and it felt good to be working towards something positive rather than trying to get away from something harmful. My neurology was so used to defending, surviving, and the notion of 'kill or be killed' that it was a new sensation to allow life to happen whilst enjoying friends, a bit of happiness, and love.

I'd kept in touch with my parents on a very casual basis; the more I was away and making my own life, the better I felt. I struggled enormously with talking to them and my own internal feelings about them. I blamed a lot on them and felt that they had 'done this' to me and wondered 'how could they?' I realised they didn't have a child-rearing manual, but neither did other parents. I had been hurt and at this point was simply suppressing that hurt, which had lain dormant for so long.

My mother had a new boyfriend called Kevin. His work was high-flying, as he was one of the top surgeons in his field and was renowned for his knowledge. He was also a raging alcoholic. Having only ever spoken to him on the phone, he was coming with my mother for a week's holiday to visit and spend time with Phil and me. As I was working and didn't have much time off, I arranged to work the morning shift all week to be able to see them as much as possible. I was excited to see them and hoped that we would have a harmonious week of fun. Neither of them having been to Perth before, they stayed in our small two bedroom unit in Wembley Downs and were welcome to make themselves at home. What transpired was something quite different.

The first morning of their visit, Kevin was drinking a bottle of whisky. He could only function in social situations with this poison inside him. Both of them treated my home like a hotel. They came and went like it was a bed and breakfast. One day I had come home at 1:30 in the afternoon ready to take them sightseeing or whatever else they wanted to do. I waited until 9:30 that night for them to come home. They told me they'd seen a movie and had dinner out. I was furious.

Kevin was rude. He was rude to my mother about her looks and thought she was ugly. My mother just sat there looking pleased with herself, as she revelled in every moment when drama was unfolding. I boiled over and told Kevin that he was absolutely never to come into my house again. I would not allow him to traipse around drunk being rude to my mother and me. I told him he was an absolute disgrace. He sat listening to me with heavy eyes and a smirk. He was swaying slightly, and I suspect that if I had pushed him with my little finger he would have plonked straight onto the floor. I earnestly wanted my mother to stand up for herself, but she said she was used to it. In that moment, I could see her lack of self-esteem. Perhaps this kind of treatment was all she knew. I felt for her. Due to her cancer, she had recently had major surgery to reconstruct her breasts, which involved twisting her back muscles around into place to form new breasts. I suspect she needed to feel whole and loved, and that was certainly not the feeling she was receiving from Kevin.

I came home in the afternoon that same week and my visitors were out, as usual. Phil was home and confided in me that something had happened whilst

I was out: Kevin had gone out to get more whisky, and he was alone with my mother. Phil told me that she had called him into her bedroom and told him about her breast surgery. She had lifted her top up and asked him to touch her breasts to see if they felt real. It's safe to say that I was absolutely furious. She was at it again, manipulating and now being sexually explicit with my boyfriend. Phil felt awful and was appalled at her behaviour. I'd had enough and wanted them out of my house. One week of visiting was enough for me. Thankfully, their visit was over, and they went back to England two damaged people living in a troubled world. Before my mother left, she told me I should lose weight. She asked me, 'When are you going to be beautiful on the outside?' Something inside me recoiled. I kept calm in the moment; though a cog was being wound up again inside my chest and another anger bubble was waiting to burst.

My father also came to visit during this time. His visit went much more swimmingly than my mother's. I was beginning to see my dad as an old man. I saw someone who had made some bad decisions in life and was now paying for them with loneliness and solitude. He was poor and at times couldn't afford to eat. Sometimes I helped out by ordering food to be delivered to his door from the local supermarket. I paid for his trips to Australia and he treated me like a princess, like there was nothing more important to him in the world than me. I treated him much the same, with respect, and although I couldn't quite reach forgiveness for the pain he had caused earlier in my life, I settled for connecting with him as a person and as a father.

Being my ever determined and spontaneous self, I approached Phil with a proposition: we should buy our very own house. Phil wasn't convinced we could afford it, but I was resolute. 'We can make anything happen if we want', I implored. He believed in me, so I withdrew all the money we had in our bank account and marched off to the first home buyers' office. Suddenly we were signed up to buy a new house in Ellenbrook, which was a new development area in the woodlands northeast of Perth, and hey presto, we were homeowners. We moved in, delighted with our new place, taking with us our cat Bobby, who got used to the area quickly.

At work, I was developing well as a team leader. Though my confidence was sometimes overbearing and my attitude somewhat entitlement-oriented, my new general manager Steve believed in me. During the time we worked together in the early 2000s, he listened to my ideas and sent me on the most fundamental leadership courses available. He encouraged me and every other staff member to be the absolute best we could be. Whilst I certainly wasn't perfect, I was learning at a rate of knots; I did my job well and cared about the people around me. However, whilst I cared, I kept people at arm's length. I didn't trust myself, let alone other people, and made sure no-one other than Phil got too close. I stopped drinking alcohol quite early on in my life, knowing that it only caused me pain and made me lose my inhibitions. I didn't want to risk doing something I would regret and generally kept myself to myself. My party days were over. I'd done my fair share anyway! Steve's belief in me and the education he afforded me gave me the most incredible and solid foundation for being a leader worth following. Whilst it took a long time for me to be able to really hone the attitude and skills I was learning at this point in my life, his encouragement helped me excel.

Rosalie, Phil's mum, decided to make another trip to see us, to see our first home and spend some time enjoying the Australian weather. She came alone this time because Anne, Phil's sister, was working in London and living with her boyfriend Richard. Rosalie arrived a happy and bubbly person, ready to explore on holiday and be with us for a few weeks. Old memories resurfaced of our difficult time in Melbourne, and I began once again to act defensively. Not yet truly consciously understanding my emotions and being ruled by unconscious triggers, I caused arguments and awkwardness once again. There were times where Rosalie returned the behaviour, being stroppy or reactive herself, though I don't blame her as I was in full form, acting up enough to test anyone's patience.

On one of the days towards the end of the visit, I told her why I loved Phil so much: he was the kindest and most generous and giving person I'd ever known. On the day Rosalie was leaving, on the way out of the house to go to the airport she took me aside and told me straight: 'Suzanne, you remember how you told me why you loved Phil so much?' 'Yes', I said. Rosalie continued, 'Well, you would do well to emulate that'.

I was aghast! I looked at her. I didn't understand what the word 'emulate' meant, but through her non-verbal signals I understood that she was telling me I wasn't like Phil, that I wasn't generous, kind, and giving. I blew my top. It felt like I was having a stroke I was so angry. I couldn't see properly and couldn't even begin to formulate words. I screamed at her to get the fuck out of my house: 'Get out, get out, get out!' Phil looked disappointed in both of us and then did what I asked: got his mother out of my house. She left to go back to England that day, leaving me a note explaining that she hadn't intended to upset me like that. Phil returned with the note after seeing her off and said we were both to blame. My anger was building again, compounding, ready to explode.

Phil and I were somewhat back to normal. Our parents had visited and returned to England, we were both doing well at work, and my old self had awoken and been triggered in my body and mind. I felt that people couldn't be trusted. I believed I could only fend for myself and that Phil was the only person I loved. I could feel myself reaching the boiling point again and knew that I was a walking time bomb. My blood felt like it was constantly boiling, and I was relentlessly heightened in my emotions. One normal weekday, Phil was in front of me on his motorbike and I was following along in my car to an appointment we both had to attend. There was a minor altercation when Phil cut in front of another driver. We had all stopped and were standing in the road. The situation escalated and Phil and the other male driver were at loggerheads with anger and rage in the middle of the road. My adrenalin was pumping. I got out of the car and calmly spoke to them, asking them to let it go and just kindly move on because the arguing wasn't worth it. The two men listened but continued to blame each other, point, and bicker; the situation remained unchanged. A rage deep inside me erupted. Like a rolling wall of red-hot hurt, it came from deep within my belly and up and out through my throat and I started to scream. I don't know the words I screamed, but it was clear I had lost my mind. I ran in front of cars driving on the road. Phil tried to calm me down, but I was a screaming mess of anger. People stared at me. The police arrived and I was asked to get in my car and calm down. Whilst the episode was over rather quickly, it was clear that my inner hurt and frustration was still incredibly raw, like a volcano ready to erupt.

A Flourishing Mind

'The illiterate of the 21st century will not be those who cannot read and write, but those who cannot learn, unlearn, and relearn.'

Alvin Toffler

Chapter 6
To Evolve or Revolve?

Phil looked after me in the following months as I recovered from my emotional explosion. I slowed down my pace of life. I was diminutively calmer after getting out the rage I'd been feeling, but I still hadn't consciously processed all my feelings from the stress I had experienced during my entire life until I saw a counsellor during these few months. The therapist helped me reflect and make some sense of what I was feeling. Approaching the year 2003, Phil and I were ready for a holiday, and since 1997 we hadn't been back to visit friends and family in England. We planned our trip for January; the snow would be coming then and I felt excited to be looking forward to something again, albeit with a little trepidation.

Rosalie was the first person on our itinerary, and she picked us up from the airport. We stayed at Rosalie's house in Bath in the south east of England for a week. This was Phil's family home, which I'd never been to. This was a welcome stopover before I departed for five days to see my mother by myself. I think being in someone else's territory at Rosalie's house helped me be more polite and less defensive. Both Rosalie and I acted as if nothing had happened the last time we had been together; she treated me with great respect and kindness, as if we needn't ever worry about the past and our previous altercation. On our first night she prepared massive sacks of presents for Christmas, treating me equally to Phil, and I felt included once again. We enjoyed the beautiful city of Bath and its surrounds. Rosalie took us far and wide, showing me Phil's early life and the beauty of the West Country. I started to understand her passion for history. The way she detailed stories of the past and her evident knowledge of her hometown were worthy of respect. I could have stayed there forever. I was feeling more connected to a family than I had for a long time. It felt like I was starting to belong. Rosalie had also arranged a large gathering of all the family I'd never met and Phil hadn't seen for many years. Surrounded by caring people and having a wonderful time, I was happy.

Moving on from Bath by train, I set out by myself for Essex to see my mother. Visiting her was far from the joy I'd experienced with Rosalie. Kevin was still drunk and my mother just moaned and sucked the life out of me with her very being. I was keen to get back to Phil and move on with our trip. One evening we went to dinner with a few people my mother had known for a long time. As we walked into the restaurant, she gushed over me and introduced me to everyone once again. I turned my head away for a moment and as I turned back towards her, I saw her indicating with her arms and puffing out her cheeks whilst gesturing her eyes and head in my direction. She was aiming this mimed display at her long-time mentor and work friend. Her action indicated that I had ballooned and put on weight. The poor guy looked appalled and slightly embarrassed, so to save confrontation I just smiled at him and chose a seat far away from my mother. Departure time soon came, and Phil and I were reunited. I was keen to move on, and soon we were on our way to visit my father in my hometown and to once again see Suzanne, my very best friend and soulmate.

Suzanne had married Colin, a previous boyfriend of mine. Colin is wonderful, and I always adored him. He's a kind, hardworking, and thoughtful person, and I was thrilled they had found each other in love. It was meant to be. In our much younger years, Colin and I, Suzanne, and Micky, her then boyfriend, were in each other's company at all hours of the day. We had great times together. Phil and I stayed at their house for a few days. Suzanne was six months pregnant and her bulging belly was so strange to me. Needless to say, we were like two peas in a pod. Colin even remarked about how it was like the two of us had never been apart. I didn't speak to her much when we were thousands of miles apart – we were more about writing letters and didn't really need to talk all the time – but our friendship prevailed. We had been through enough to be joined together forever, much like I was with her family. Seeing Suzanne reminded me that another type of family exists: the type you can choose that never goes away. During our stay, Phil and I continued to holiday and visited old haunts, such as Eastwell Manor, where most of the people we had known there had moved on – apart from Hugo, the resident cat, who still liked to flop himself in front of the roaring fire in the grand main hall.

Returning to Australia exhausted from cold England, we were happy to be home, and I continued life more relaxed and at peace with the world. Phil and I were soulmates too; even though we had both changed throughout the years, we always grew together, even when we grew in different directions. We were abundant in our determination at working through communication so as to come back into parallel with each other.

Whilst Phil remained in his role, building his professional skills as an executive chef, I changed jobs a few times, building my own skills in the HR and training field, including my leadership skills, and combining knowledge that gave me all-round experience. Having such a rapidly changing life at an early age, I had never stuck with a job for more than three years and found it hard to feel motivated after that amount of time. I wanted new and constant change to appease what I was unconsciously searching for – satisfaction. Phil and I moved to a new apartment closer to the city, a modern and beautiful place where he surprised me one evening and asked me to marry him. Having been together for seven years, finally, after lots of asking from me, he had decided it was time. We didn't know if we believed in marriage *per se*, though we did want to have a day where we all came together to celebrate and love each other, and we decided to do that in the form of a wedding after all.

Life was amazing. For the most part, I felt like a fog had lifted from my world, and I felt freer than I ever had before. Phil and I were doing well financially and growing our worth in that area. We moved into a stunning property in the hills of Perth. Our house was situated up high, looking out at the bottom of our tree-lined road over the city sparkling far off in the distance. At the back of our land was a stream that meandered through all the properties on our street. Guarding the stream was a bridge and a small platform where wildlife and humans alike could sit and ponder the ways of the world. Towards the left and down some steps a thirty-year-old grapevine wound its way through an awning over a green mosaic table that could seat twelve people. Hidden in the trees, plants, and walls sat a serene blue swimming pool that kept the place cool. It was beautiful. I cried when I first saw it, and Phil, having seen many properties in his search, said that this one was by far the best out of all the properties he'd viewed. A perfect place for a wedding, wouldn't you agree?

Ironically, I worked an hour's drive down the hill near the apartment we'd just sold. Working as a training and HR coordinator, I was flying around the country, training and supporting new franchise owners of a printing company in running their small businesses. I learned a lot about business in that job, and bringing my people skills together with my business skills was a good balance. To date, my managers had been supportive and mostly easy to get along with. The manager at this role was the opposite. At this point in my life I had never met such an emotional wreck in the workplace! As she worked in Melbourne and I in Perth, we were bound to each other through a partnership over the phone.

Having a lot of personal difficulties in her own life with her husband, she drank a lot, worked even more, and was a walking needy mess of confusion. She was great at her job, but her people skills left a lot to be desired. My resolve was tested with her constant barking on the phone. Her frequent crying in front of our franchise owners and her whining about how she knew she treated me badly but couldn't help it was exasperating. The whole company was a mess. The CEO wasn't respected and the place was riddled with infighting and gossip.

The majority of my friends today come from this time in my life, as we all endured such a difficult time and we were forced to bond. It wasn't the best form of team building, but it worked! The thing I love about these difficult situations is that you learn to build your own standards and expectations of yourself. Whilst I didn't fully know who or what I wanted to be or do in life, I knew what I didn't want to be; I didn't want to be like my current boss: sad, angry, disliked, and lost. How is that a life worth living? My friends from this job all came from different departments, such as finance, marketing, IT and administration, and I am honoured to have remained friends with them for years. My own network of support and community was beginning to expand.

We bonded so well that Sarah, the strategic markets manager, soon became a dear friend. She was a crazy, wild, blonde, curly-haired woman with confidence to match her wild hair. It's ironic, really, that at first

I didn't really warm to her. She was demanding and quite direct in the office. It was on a trip to Cairns and Port Douglas that we bonded on the aeroplane. We worked hard together at hosting a conference for hundreds of people, and we realised we were friends – we had earned each other's respect. I only had a few people in my life at that point; most of my old friends had dropped off the radar. I wasn't good at keeping relationships intact and disregarded people who didn't live up to my expectations. Sarah was an exception. She became my friend and later my bridesmaid, and she is a very dear friend to this day. I also met Melinda, Cheryl, and Jeff, who have become solid parts of my life. Our friendships have bloomed and I treasure them all dearly. I trust these people. They showed me the meaning of trust whilst the rest of the business we worked in crumbled around us due to poor management. I recognised that I was starting to learn to let people in. I was learning that not everyone has a hidden agenda, that not everyone was manipulating me. I was getting better and realising that people make mistakes and I am not the judge and jury.

During my time in this role, being in my late twenties and more settled than I'd ever been, I decided to become a crisis counsellor at Lifeline WA, a charitable organisation that helped people in crisis, including domestic violence, suicide, loneliness – the list goes on. I worked hard for years volunteering and supporting troubled Australians with their problems over the telephone. During that time I learned a lot about how to cope, how to teach others to cope, and the basics of human behaviour. I became qualified as a crisis counsellor and added another skill to my ever-growing list of capabilities.

Volunteering there humbled me. I had experienced a lot of heartache in my life, and to be able to do now what those other people did for me in my time of need, extending an unbiased hand, was truly rewarding. I didn't get caught up in other people's problems like other volunteers did. I had learned to disconnect my feelings at an early age to protect myself, so I was considered a good asset to the organisation with my ability to be empathetic and my experience with crisis.

In April 2007, Phil and I were married. Regardless of my somewhat difficult time at work, life was wonderful. I had friends and a beautiful house, I was in love with my new husband, and I felt like I was a jigsaw puzzle being put back together to show a stunning picture. People came from England to join us and we had a small wedding of thirty people in our garden on a warm, breezy Friday afternoon. The day was magnificent; everything went according to plan. Phil and I felt like we were a king and queen, and it was made all the more special by having all the special people in our lives congregated in one place.

At one stage I looked out of our kitchen window days before the wedding and saw Robyn from Melbourne happily pottering in the garden tidying and weeding. My father was sitting reading his book, Rosalie and Anne were talking in the sun, and other people were milling around generally getting excited about the wedding that was about to take place. A feeling of community was in the air. My next-door neighbours, who were like grandparents to me, offered their small granny flat to my mother and Robyn to stay in together. Phil's aunty and some others in his family stayed in our spare rooms, as did my father. Our house was full to the breaking point with Phil's sister and boyfriend in the last spare room and Rosalie camped out in the office!

Two days before the wedding, our neighbour Jenny, who was seventy years old, approached me with some worrying news. As my mother and Robyn had been staying in her granny flat, she'd seen more of them than I had so far, and she had been cornered by my mother. Being very progressive people and incredibly positive influences on many lives in our community, Jenny and her husband were able to recognise my mother's victim mentality and weren't very impressed with her – they didn't buy into her games.

According to Jenny, my mother had told her she planned to kill herself whilst at our home. Looking at Jenny with a mild amount of surprise, I found myself saying, 'Thanks, Jenny, we'll cross that bridge when we come to it'. I'd heard it all before and wasn't going to play the game. Jenny instinctively understood and left it at that. Of course, I shared all this with Phil, who had lost all respect for my mother many years ago and wouldn't tolerate her. She even reduced him to shouting when she continuously badgered him about nonsense that was simply about seeking his attention. Of course, shouting at her just fuelled her victim mentality, and she used this to create drama to anyone that listened about the fact that Phil doesn't like her, she isn't good enough, and so on and so on. What was it that kept me in the relationship? In a lot of ways, I am a patient person. I wanted to have a mother, to have a relationship with this woman who hadn't been in my life in any meaningful way.

The night before the wedding, after our rehearsal with Phil's best man and Sarah as bridesmaid, a dinner was prepared at Sarah's house – the last feast. As I was staying at Sarah's house, my mother stayed back with me whilst the other ladies left to get ready for the next day back at my home. Sitting out in the fresh air with a little blanket over our knees, my mother and I sat talking whilst Sarah kindly cleared up the plates in the kitchen. I'd told Sarah a lot about what my mother was like, and she had patiently listened over the years, though she'd never seen her in action.

Listening in to the conversation from afar, she heard my mother take the chance to once again attempt to coerce me and manipulate me by repeatedly going over old stories. She was intent on talking about the times when I was a child and my father hit me, or on insisting that Sara really did try to poison me, or that all she had was the clothes on her back when my dad cheated on her. She would have given me anything, even those clothes from her back. She continued to declare how Phil was wonderful and how she would never find anyone to love her the way he loved me.

Sarah couldn't hide her shock. She stood in the doorway lit only by the house lights, as the sun was almost completely set, shaking her head in dismay. I was familiar with this behaviour, disappointed but never surprised, so I politely asked my mother to just stop talking. I encouraged her to savour this moment between us on the eve of my wedding and to be happy.

She was only there for four days. Kevin wasn't invited to the wedding as he'd been banned from last time. She announced to me that she couldn't come for any longer than four days, as her horse would miss her too much. Her horse! Realising she couldn't bait me, her victim needs unmet, she went back to my home, leaving Sarah and I to spend the last hours of the night together.

As I'm sure you can imagine, having my father, mother, and Phil's mother in one house together was nerve-racking. My father, being his crass and inappropriate cringe-worthy self, said things to Phil's mother that made me want to slap him. I was embarrassed, and I think he knew it. He was old school, old and rough. His heart was in the right place, however, and I knew this. He even stopped smoking for the wedding, as he knew we didn't smoke and didn't want it to be an issue. He put himself out to try to fit in, though he was still a stark difference to Rosalie, who was an upstanding, churchgoing member of her community!

The day of our marriage was remarkable. Marrying Phil was a day like no other. The grounds of the house were immaculate, with flowers and nature all around us. Our friends were in high spirits. Our family were all there to see us come together formally and declare our love. Dancing, laughing, and loving were the order of the day. I wouldn't have changed a single thing. The day after the wedding, the newlywed husband and wife arrived back from our wedding night hotel. We'd had a chance to relax and enjoy the moments and memory of the best day of my life. It was such fun having the night to ourselves, lounging and reflecting on the wonderful day we'd experienced. I walked into our house and was greeted by my mother scrambling to get to me and tell me that my father had been spreading lies whilst I was gone. She started to tell me that he was saying she had gone bankrupt and not him. I just took one look at my mother-in-law with a look that implored 'please get her away from me', and she mercifully jumped into action and removed my mother from my sight.

We had literally just walked into the house and my mother was still causing drama. I think Rosalie finally understood why I was the way I was years ago. She and I were now allies, and I thank her every day for being gracious and teaching her son good morals and values, who in turn showed me what it means to be respectful and kind. Finally, it was time for my mother to go home, and I took her to the airport. Sitting in a café a couple of days after my wedding, saying goodbye, my mother began once again to dramatically expose to me that she didn't think I needed her anymore, that I had my own life with someone who loved me. She carried on in this vein and I truly don't remember the shocking thing she said next.

I remember it was very shocking; I recall sitting there in shock, feeling hot with that feeling of red in my heart and insane disappointment. I was aware that I had a choice right then never to speak to her again and to cut her off for good. Would I do it? Could I do it? I just didn't want to hurt anyone. So, in the middle of her speech, to save myself and stop this nonsense, I got up and told her to have a good flight, thanks for coming, and walked off! I simply drove home in the dark, feeling strangely both livid and calm. I got home to bed at 1:00 a.m. and promptly erased from my memory what she had said to me. To this day, all I know is that what she said hurt so much that I disconnected just that little bit more from her. I didn't stop speaking to her, but I did withdraw from our relationship.

I was married and happy and everyone was back where they had come from. Phil's sister and boyfriend decided to immigrate to Perth and settle. Not long after them, Rosalie moved to Perth, too, leaving her sixty-something years of friends and familiarity to join her children. After living in the hills at our beautiful property for a few years, in 2008 we decided the work required for its upkeep was too much. We found ourselves cleaning, mowing, and doing handy work when we should have been relaxing and enjoying the very things we were slaves to. We had made a fortune in the housing boom from all our properties up to then, and this one was no different. With money to spend, we moved back down the hill closer to the city into a modern townhouse with four bedrooms, a courtyard, and much less maintenance.

Leaving my tumultuous role with the mad manager, I accepted a promoted position at a major market share insurance company as an operations coordinator. With more money, more responsibility, and more people to work with, I was in heaven leading leaders and their teams. I was soon to be promoted to claims manager with a department that had in excess of seventy employees and millions of dollars to work with in the cost centre. I loved my job and thoroughly enjoyed my confidence and my ability to influence and get good results at work. I put my heart and soul into my work. I had stable friends who I enjoyed being around and a husband who was still happy and successful at his job. I had tasted what it was like to have nice things, choices in life, and the ability to create your own reputation and results. I was finally becoming satisfied.

A tremendous bombshell hit in 2009 when I connected with an old friend on Facebook – the same friend who had gone upstairs with my dad that night years ago when we were ten years old. I'd always wondered about that night and what it really meant, and now I had an opportunity to find out from her what had happened. She had grown up through tough times herself and now worked as a rape and crisis counsellor helping other women. She had two children and still lived not far from our childhood hometown. In the private message section of Facebook I asked her directly and gently whether what I remembered had really happened.

She replied and told me the entire story, how my father had sexually abused her for nearly three years. Between the ages of ten and thirteen, she would go from school to our house or she would stay over with us and he would get her to touch him sexually. I asked if he ever touched her, and she said that he did a few times but didn't seem comfortable with it. I was absolutely beside myself with hurt, shame, and fear. My friend was being very careful with me in her words and treated me with respect, as I did her. I believed her completely. I remember the night myself.

My other friends were often very uncomfortable in my father's presence, as for as long as I can remember he often tried to get them to sit on his lap so he could tickle them. Other dads didn't do that.

After much consoling from Phil and Rosalie, I decided to confront my father over the telephone, as he was at his home in England. Alone in the bedroom, I made the call. I couldn't believe my own voice. It was like steel, hard and purposeful. Much like when I had asked him all those years ago, I confronted my father once more and asked if he had indeed molested my friend for three years. He raised his voice as if three years was far too long – 'three years'! To me, this was a sign of admission of guilt, as he didn't deny it but only denied the time frame. So I asked him, 'If it wasn't for three years, how long did it go on for?' He went silent. I asked again. He said, 'Please don't'.

I brought up the fact that he was with Sara when she was a teenager and asked how that was much different. I asked him about another young girl he was close to who was currently in his life. He was appalled, absolutely disgusted, that I'd suggest that he would do such a heinous thing to this girl. I caught him out, saying, 'But you don't think it's disgusting to do it to my friend?' He was silent again, and again he didn't defend himself. I knew it was true. I asked him to be absolutely truthful with me. Lying would be worse than telling the truth at this point. I'd had enough lies in my life. I worked better when I knew where I stood.

I pleaded with him. I could hear the contemplation of his confession in his silence. He said nothing. I continued and said that I'd have to think about this and how I felt about what would happen next. He was almost whimpering on the phone, pleading with me not to leave him. He couldn't live without me; he had nothing if he didn't have me. He actually said that if he didn't have me in his life he might as well jump off a cliff. I hung up the phone and was shell-shocked. I didn't get a confession, but I may as well have. This was real. Having dealt with many people who had committed sexual offences at Lifeline, I understood that it's rarely as simple as it seems.

Some people do bad things because of bad circumstances, though not everyone. Some people manage to cope and work their way through situations whilst others succumb to their demons. I believe my father paid for this sin his whole life. I thought about who he is now, who my friend is now, and how her life is perfectly good and happy. I considered his life of loneliness, his not being able to afford food and scaring off many who loved him because of his petty and controlling ways. Forgiveness and understanding felt right. Compassion and thinking of the bigger picture was apt. He was an old man in his sixties who had nothing but his daughter. I just wouldn't cut him off. I did decide that I would make it very clear that I knew what had happened and that we would need to work to get trust and respect back, if it was possible at all.

After some time thinking about this decision, I called him again. He answered the phone with anticipation and panic in his voice, and I explained my thinking in a rational and calm way. I was completely in control, thinking clearly, and knew that this was a new me. I was becoming able to cope with and control my emotions even in the most difficult circumstances.

I could see outside of myself and think about the impact of my actions and other people's situations, and it felt empowering. My father actually thanked me, and though our relationship was different from that point on, it had an underlying restraint to it. We continued to communicate and interact. Frankly, the ball was always in my court from there on out. I used it wisely and didn't take advantage, and he would never again be rude or petty with me or anyone else for the matter.

'You cannot control what happens to you, but you can control your attitude toward what happens to you, and in that, you will be mastering change rather than allowing it to master you.'

Brian Tracy

Chapter 7
Alive & Kicking

During my time as a manager, the business I worked at experienced a major catastrophe. A freak hailstorm caused almost one year's worth of insurance claims to be made in just one afternoon. Several months into this crisis, my team were still working long and hard hours. The stress of continuing customer complaints started to creep into the language they used, and their lack of tolerance of customers and each other was showing. It seemed like there was no end in sight, and they were drained. I too had worked incredibly hard, often in excess of ninety hours a week. I was reliable, capable, and working incredibly well.

To support the team in this challenge, I enlisted the services of a specialist team that would provide stress management and effective communication skills training. I'd heard about the company years before. I used to know one of the owners, but since then he had apparently moved on, leaving just one owner who I'd actually met once before. The business' reputation preceded it. They had gained a strong name for themselves, so without much need for research, I called them to schedule an appointment. After meeting with Fran Berry, the founder and now sole owner of *Alive & Kicking Solutions*, about the training, we signed up immediately. We started with a pilot project that would provide our people with the emotional support they needed – and quickly.

After seeing Fran in action during the training, I was astonished. She had had so many experiences in life and real success helping people who worked in the corporate world think critically and communicate with genuine passion. Working with the likes of Robert Kiyosaki and Anthony Robbins, she had some major education and knowledge about human behaviour – and I wanted to know more. How did such a woman exist? Where did she learn all of this? We had been getting on really well in our short communications with each other, and one afternoon when packing up from a day of working with my team I plucked up the courage to ask Fran if we could get to know each other more. I wanted to learn from her. I asked her if she wanted to set a time to go to dinner sometime during the week. She looked at me with one eyebrow raised and in her American accent said, 'Why, you wanna come and play?' The meaning of the question wasn't lost on me. She was interested in working with me, and I hadn't even considered that this could or would be a possibility.

I now remember about ten years prior to this day that, ironically, Fran's business partner and I were co-facilitating a presentation as part of a committee we both supported. I remember that during that experience I longed to be able to do what he did. I wanted the skills he displayed, the knowledge he had. I wanted to help others be better versions of themselves, just like he did. I just didn't have enough experience or knowledge at the time to pull it off. But I knew back then that it was a dream. I didn't want to be a psychologist or a doctor; I wanted to work with people and support them in a non-clinical way. Knowing that I had her interest now after all this time was extraordinary. I was finally in a position to be noticed and regarded as worth having a conversation with about my career. Fran and I went to dinner and got to know each other both personally and professionally.

After three dinners, lots of conversation, and meeting my husband, Phil, Fran made it clear to me that the door was open for me to join the company and it was now up to me to decide. I was thrilled, flattered, and petrified. I had worked insanely hard to get where I was – in a senior leadership role – and now I was considering giving it all up. I couldn't believe it. Phil and I talked at length about the opportunities this role would give me and us, but I was not used to working at a small company, working from home, and working with a 'cash flow is king' mentality. What if we didn't make enough money and it couldn't go on anymore? What if I wasn't any good at what Fran was so excellent at? Then I started to consider: no staff, no budgets, and no constant days of meetings. Just working with people on a deep level to support them in making positive changes in their life and at work. Ah, yes. That's it. I'm sold. People. No more insurance or the politics of a big organisation, and no more restrictions! I considered, reflected, and waited for three weeks before I decided to take the job.

One night, after being completely silent all night (which in my world means I'm extremely stressed), I suddenly rose up out of my sofa, strode to the phone, and called Fran to accept her offer. She screamed into the phone with excitement and I resigned from my job that very week. I gave two months notice, as I had yet another surgical operation scheduled for my endometriosis, my ninth operation, to help clean and separate my organs, which were twisted together because of the disease. My manager at the insurance company was impressed and said that it 'took balls to follow a dream' – and he was right. It did, even if secretly I still wasn't consciously sure what the dream was!

Alive & Kicking Solutions was born in the early 2000s and had been around for some time, supporting businesses and their individuals to communicate truly, authentically and effectively, to understand their own environments, their emotional triggers, and how to manage themselves when communicating. Leadership and coaching frameworks were taught to help leaders lead with inspiration and empowerment, and I loved every moment of my own journey. Learning to facilitate and train under Fran was a confronting, supportive, and expansive journey. She used methods I'd never heard of before, such as NLP (Neuro-Linguistic Programming), and her training style was unique and energetic. It was unlike anything I'd seen in the corporate world or anywhere else before.

To work with *Alive & Kicking*, you need to uncover who you are and what you believe in and then be ready to accept that you have the absolute ability to change your own circumstances. I had experienced a lot in my life so far and been through so many situations both positive and negative. I recognised that I was still sorting and working out my reason for being. What was I put on this Earth for? The million-dollar question: why do we exist? Now in my thirties, I was a long way away from the old promiscuous trouble-seeking me of my youth. I'd proven myself able to work hard and endure, to persist and grow in life, love, and work. Phil and I were happier than ever, and the more I was at peace with myself – accepting and understanding the traumas I'd experienced early on – the more opportunities opened up to me.

Fran encouraged me to explore, push boundaries, and create my own role in her company. She opened my eyes to true empowerment and trust as an employer and gave me the scope to be and do whatever felt right. I created an entire sales and marketing arm of the business that hadn't existed before, which left me with the realisation of how strategic I am. In other jobs, I'd been repeatedly told I was not strategic and that I needed to grow those skills. I had started to believe those people. I realise upon reflection that I was indeed very strategic, I just didn't believe in myself, so those people didn't either. Now I was in an environment where learning, growing, and experimenting was encouraged – and I thrived. Work wasn't work anymore – it was play. I worked longer hours and harder than I ever had before. Meeting different clients at their workplaces, consulting on performance and motivation for staff, and training, facilitating, and growing a new arm of the business meant I had so much variety in my day. I was constantly fulfilled, raring to go every morning, ready for the day with so much energy and enthusiasm. I also soon came to realise that I am an incredibly 'high change' person. I need lots of variety and change to feel motivated, and this role became my passion. I was addicted, obsessed, and absolutely loving every moment of my life.

Early on in my working career, I was prone to calling in sick, using up my sick days and other leave because I was 'owed' it. I used to leave on time, raring to 'finish' and get home to my real life outside the office. At *Alive & Kicking*, I was never finished and days did not end. They rolled into each other gloriously. In the entire time I have worked at *Alive & Kicking* I have taken no more than a few sick days off over the years because 'sick' only happens now if I catch it. I'm healthier because I found something I believe in. I wanted to be there. I wanted to improve the lives of the people we worked with, and nothing was going to get in my way.

As time went on, Fran taught me how to create what I want in life rather than waiting for it to 'happen to me'. She played board games with Phil and I that were designed to help people learn. She taught us about investing in property and managing money effectively. My mind was on fire with all the possibilities, and I'd finally found what I was looking for: someone to teach me how to create, on purpose, my own life. Teaching other people these strategies, tools, and techniques in the corporate world was challenging at times because the people involved were often institutionalised, bound by societal thinking, focused on what can't be done rather than what can. I began to realise that this was just a matter of knowledge, of understanding the options, and my own mission started to be born. I too had a dream that people can do anything they want, they just hadn't been taught how to achieve that type of thinking yet.

My co-worker Beth was equally inspirational and was my running mate within the team. At first we spent our time figuring out how best to work with each other, as we were both strong and upfront people and needed to find our places in the new working arrangement. We became very close. In fact, when Beth left to work as a general manager at another business in Perth, as it was her time to grow and expand in her career, our friendship became even stronger. Being surrounded by people who influenced me in this positive way was remarkable and taught me the power of exposure. What we expose ourselves to is what we ultimately become. Put simply, 'we are what we think about all day long'.

Having learned the basics of NLP through Fran, I had a strong desire to understand and know more. I wanted to experience and get qualified for myself, so I decided to go to a taster weekend to see what NLP was all about. I found a weekend course that gave participants a chance to get a feel for NLP without going through the whole course. Fran was thrilled that there was a place with training of this quality in Perth. I suggested to my teammates that we all go and experience it together. A whole weekend with a hundred or so people in a big room in the city was exhilarating. We were exposed to the directors and trainers of the company whose training weekend we were attending, namely Wilbert Molenaar (from the Netherlands) and Grace Minton (from Perth, Australia), NLP and coach master trainers. Having never really been exposed to this type of environment – where the whole aim of the course is to learn about oneself, improve oneself, and become aware of how to live your life the way you want to – I was equally overwhelmed and convinced. I wanted to become qualified, and so did my teammates. We met with Fran and explained that we wanted to spend ten thousand dollars of the company's money to put us all through a sixteen-day NLP practitioner course that ran over several months. Fran immediately agreed. In fact, I don't ever recall Fran saying 'No' to anything. She always said 'Yes' and then 'How?' Another great saying of Fran's is that if money is the only problem, there isn't a problem. She believes that all that is needed is a plan and a solution to create the money. So Beth negotiated with Grace for a discount for our signing up three people at once. We were on our way to start the training in 2011!

Wilbert, a Dutch guy who admittedly speaks 'D'inglish' – a mixture of Dutch and English – along with Grace, who was born and bred in Western Australia, took us through the most intense learning experience of my life. Over sixteen gut-wrenching, heartwarming, and mind-opening days, we were safely exposed to understanding how humans work. Of course, to truly understand the inner workings of the human species we needed to start with ourselves. In order to truly be able to understand and support one another, we must first know ourselves. Opening myself up in a raw and transparent manner had never been something I did. I protected myself. I was lovely, friendly, and open with people, but it was all within my control. I was never truly vulnerable or exposed, except with Phil. At the end of the course, we were tested on our knowledge by having to answer questions and demonstrate live practitioner coaching with our assessor. At the finale, when I had passed my exams and was asked what I'd learned, I answered, 'I've learned that I have a lot more to learn!' We finished the course and I still longed for more. I'd found my passion at an even deeper level and I yearned to learn as much as I could – these principles and fundamental human ways of being appealed to me greatly. It was as though I'd found the map of how humans work and how I worked, and I knew I could help people more than ever by getting as much knowledge as I could.

Having finished high school with very average grades, I believed that I couldn't go to university and succeed because I just wasn't clever enough. These shorter qualifications (crisis counselling and NLP) were perfect for me. I was relieved that there was a way to learn and become qualified in something I loved and that I knew would enhance my career as a human behavioural expert. I was searching for further courses when one day a stranger in an unrelated meeting proclaimed that it would do me good to study a tertiary degree and said he felt I would learn so much. I was tempted to follow the advice but had this limiting belief that I couldn't do it. Phil, as always, believed that I could do anything and knew that once I set my mind to something I was bound to achieve it. I didn't believe him. Tempted, I researched the topic further and asked questions of the different universities, working out how much it would cost and how much time would be involved.

During my research, I came across the very people I had studied NLP with. I discovered that they were offering a master's degree in applied coaching. Reading about the program, I was hooked: it was exactly what I wanted to learn. Over three years, combining NLP and coaching studies, I would learn how to support people individually and in groups, how to change their thinking, generate positive thoughts, and help them live their lives on purpose. It was perfect. But the same old limiting belief sprung up - a university degree? How would I ever be able to do this? As always, I turned to my wonderful friend Fran, my boss, and asked for her advice. She loved the idea. I had more excuses. I can't afford it. Will I be able to study academically? Fran's view was that you can learn to learn. Learning is just another strategy. I was becoming more and more convinced that I wanted to do it, but 'how' was another story altogether.

One day I received a call from Fran out of the blue. She wanted to come over and tell me something special. I was excited to hear her news. Sitting at my dinner table with our computers out and ready to do some work together, Fran announced that she would like to personally pay for my master's degree and that she would like to join me and do it too! I was overcome. Fran wanted to show me how valued I was in her company. She knew that paying for the master's would open up so many opportunities, both for me and for her own business. Our new knowledge journey together was an exciting chance to add yet another arm to the business, and I would become more and more powerful with my skill set. It was amazing, and I felt very emotional that this wonderful woman believed in me enough to want to personally sponsor me.

A Flourishing Mind

Being strategic, I said yes, and on one condition: that we find a way to pay for the degree through the business, as we could write it off for tax purposes. We knew we could always fall back on Fran's personal money if necessary, and she agreed. I also wanted to add one more condition: that I would not have any pay rises until the degree was finished. The degree was my way of being rewarded, and it was more than enough. We made a deal and started our journey of several years of studying, writing, and researching whilst working hard and building our combined and separate dreams.

Studying with Wilbert and Grace for my master's degree was an amazing experience. We had other teachers fly in from England to teach us the subjects they were qualified in. Wilbert and Grace also entered into our cohort, so our teachers became our study mates. New deep and meaningful friendships were born. My relationship with Wilbert grew into something incredibly special, as we had shared so many of my raw and deep experiences together. Learning to hold myself in difficult times and be truly open to life without protecting, controlling, or creating perceived barriers takes an enormous amount of energy, and I was committed to this quest. Wilbert supported me every step of the way without judgement, even though I sometimes pushed him to the limit! I've never met such an amazing man to learn from. Because of these people I was exposed to and worked so closely with, I finally started to realise what I am truly capable of. I uncovered what I stand for, what I believe in, and who I am.

My father and mother were still in England. I kept in contact with them and had been working through my relationship with them on this learning journey with my own coaches and in class. I worked on forgiving and understanding my parents to allow me to be at peace with myself and not have lingering regrets or hurt that would ultimately only affect me and my quality of life. Feeling ready to see my parents again after a long time apart, Phil and I agreed that I would go back to England by myself to spend time with my mother, father and my friend Suzanne for a month's holiday. I'd been Skypeing with my mother frequently and we'd been getting on quite well, so I was actually looking forward to seeing her more than ever before. She had been whinging less and had been generally more positive over the past year. Furthermore, having moved to the countryside in Cambridgeshire with Kevin to their own small private equestrian centre, retired and enjoying life, she seemed to have found her own groove.

So in June, which is summertime in England, I took a month off from *Alive & Kicking* and my studies and set off to visit my home country, my family, and my friends. After a long but easy flight, I arrived at Heathrow airport. My mother and Kevin were waiting at the gate for me, and I was excited to see them as I walked expectantly through the doors. My mother looked a bit anxious, so I gave her a great big cuddle, which she seemed a little taken aback by. Kevin was smiling, so I greeted him warmly too. Being smokers, they were desperate to get outside and had waited a long time to see me. I associated her jitters with needing her nicotine fix.

We started the long drive to Cambridgeshire along car-packed motorways before easing into the countryside after a couple of hours of travelling. In the car we talked about small, generic things, and we were just getting used to being together after such a long time apart. Arriving at their new home was fantastic; I got to see the beautiful countryside and the stunning house and equestrian centre my mother had told me so much about. We had seven days together, with plans to visit my mother's father, my grandad, and explore the little townships around their new home. Never one to waste a moment, I was ready for action immediately, wanting to go into town the next day. The night of my arrival started busily. I unpacked and washed the clothes I'd worn on the plane because they were the only clothes appropriate to wear around horses and the mini-farm, I wanted to refresh them as soon as I could. Unexpectedly, my mother was already making snide little comments to Kevin when she thought I couldn't hear her about how I'd only just got here and was 'making' her do my washing. I just ignored her and let it go, putting my new-found emotional control techniques into practice.

I woke up the next morning ready for adventure and to spend time with my mother and Kevin only to find them out and about already in the front garden chopping down a tree. Watching them through the window, I helped myself to breakfast and sat in the unfamiliar kitchen, surveying the area. Toward midmorning, I put on some clothes and went outside to see what they were up to. It seemed they had set themselves a target to complete this task today. I was a bit taken aback, as having flown over from Australia

I expected to at least do some things together, and not for them to be tackling jobs that could be done next week when I was gone. The blacksmith was due to come in the afternoon to sort out the horseshoes, so my mother couldn't go into town to help me get a UK SIM card for my phone. Kevin kindly said he'd take me, my mother wasn't impressed and started to moan about always being left out. I quickly suggested we wait until after the blacksmith had come or until the next day, but my mother insisted she was used to being left behind and that we should go.

Of course, identifying her victim status once more, I didn't want to play the game. Knowing that she was completely responsible for her own state of mind and her own actions, as we all are, I decided to call her bluff and agreed to go with Kevin for the afternoon. Honestly, we had a great time, sorting out changing my money, getting a SIM card, looking in shops, laughing at casual passers-by, buying bread for dinner, and having coffee in the café on the high street. Back home we were full of fun and stories of our few hours of adventure, in which my mother was not interested or impressed and quickly dismissed it all. The week went on in much the same vein. Every chance she got to do something on the farm without me, she took. I toughed it out and tried to help, but she was much more used to manual work than I was. I felt like a nuisance, and it was obvious that we had grown apart even more than I'd thought. Kevin, on the other hand, after all this time and his extremely poor behaviour previously, was my saviour. He constantly made sure I felt welcome and offered to do things together, for which I was very grateful.

After days of continuous whinging and subtle but consistently negative comments and attempts at attention-seeking manipulation, I finally lost it in the car with my mother on the way to a garden centre. I blurted out at the top of my voice whilst crying that I'd never met someone so ungrateful, who moans and finds wrong in everything that happens. I exclaimed that she created her own life and for everything she hated and for everything that happened to her, she was responsible for her reaction to it. I confessed that I was thinking about leaving that night and that I didn't deserve to be treated this way. I had spent a lot of money and time to come and be with her and I'd had enough.

She pulled the car over to the side of the road, the wipers swishing with the rain starting to come down hard, and looked satisfied with herself. Of course, drama is what she knew and lived for. She listened to me calmly and took what I had to say on board, saying I should do what I thought was best, and we drove on to the garden centre, even though I wanted to be driven back to her house. This is a typical manipulator response. The manipulator drives the situation to a head and when the eruption happens, becomes calm and knowing. I reconginsed it straight away. When we arrived at the centre I asked her to give me some privacy so I could call Phil from my phone to talk to him about what I should do. He was amazing, as always, and completely supportive. He wasn't surprised at the call. His advice was to be true to myself and act with integrity. He said that if I wanted to leave, I should do so, and it would be OK. Conversely, it was OK to stay and stick it out to see if things would improve. The most important thing, he said, was that I should do what seemed right in my heart because I could do anything.

After calming down and listening to my inner voice, I joined my mother in the garden centre, where I found her looking at hanging baskets. I suggested we go and have a coffee and talk about the situation. We bought our drinks and sat on high stools overlooking the gift area in the garden centre. Gently confronting my mother, I explained again how I felt and how I didn't like the way she'd been acting. She openly admitted that she never felt she could be a mother to me and that she thought I didn't need her. She shared that every time she looked at me she felt hatred because she saw my father in me. Well, at least I knew how she really felt! I told her directly that I didn't need her to be my mother. I wanted to get to know her properly without the constant dredging up of the past and moaning about life. I gave her permission to let go of the notion of being my mother if that was what she wanted.

She admitted that I scared the hell out of her, and then she dropped a bombshell, saying that she couldn't forgive the fact that I chose my father over her when I was seven years old. I had no clue what she was talking about – so I asked her. After her unclear answer I can still only assume she was talking about the time I had a nervous breakdown and went from my foster family to my father's house. How she possibly thinks I chose that I have no idea. A mass of disappointment sat in the pit of my stomach. It was no longer disappointment for me, but for her. To be still clinging onto a distorted view of the past with only blame and self-pity for fuel is a waste of a life. At that exact moment I had a feeling of peace with myself, an inner confidence that I was a good person, and I just let it all go. I put her first and saw beyond just me. I told her that this was all behind us now, that we should focus on enjoying this week and not wasting the chance to change things into a positive, happy experience, and that we should get on with it – together. She agreed and we pottered around the garden centre, looking for something we could create or make together in the few days we had left.

Sadly, this momentary feeling of acceptance between us was fleeting, and the next few days were as hellish as the previous ones. My mother concocted a story that she couldn't get in touch with my grandad over the phone. She said that because it was a three-hour drive to his house each way, she didn't want to go that far only for him not to be there, so we didn't go. She said she'd rather spend the petrol money on clothes for herself. She suggested we go shopping instead. I know this action was concocted because my Aunty Chris – one of my mother's four sisters, the only one I knew who was in contact with my mother – called later that week and said that my grandad had been expecting us and asked why we hadn't gone. This sort of behaviour in my life wasn't unusual, as there had been plenty of occasions when my mother had been caught lying. Other instances were revealed, such as her telling me she had been visiting my grandad every month when I found out later that she hadn't seen him in years.

Another example of her lying was when she was ill with cancer when I was very young. She had been telling my father's friend Nicki that he would leave her in the bath when she couldn't look after herself or even get out of the bath by herself, leaving her stuck there with me crying as a baby in nappies. None of it was true.

I made the best call I could at the time and just got on with it, ready to leave as soon as my departure date arrived. We ventured out to a cathedral and to Cambridge in the final days, largely at Kevin's insistence, as my mother didn't want to do anything but be with her horse. I was raring to go and do something. I really enjoyed my time with Kevin, who was much changed. He was still drinking and an alcoholic, but he was keeping it much more in check. My mother, acting much like a teenager, not wanting to participate and getting stroppy on our trips, stayed out of my way, and I just got on with my visit, enjoying what I could and counting down the days until I left. On the final night, Kevin had invited some new friends of theirs to dinner at a local pub to celebrate my trip. Their friends were excited to meet me and it was nice to actually go out somewhere in the evening.

Before we left that night, my mother started fretting, and I asked her what was wrong. She said she knew what would happen when we were out, that Kevin would try to have affairs with the bar staff and would get drunk and be rude to her. I tried to assure her that it would be OK and that we would work out any problems if and when they happened. I wasn't entirely at odds with her worries, as I had seen him act atrociously before. It's safe to say that none of her worries came true, even though she believes they did, imagining Kevin flirting with the waitresses when he was just being friendly.

We got to the pub, which was a typical old beauty in the countryside with roaring fires and hearty food. Laughing faces from the other patrons and the bar staff greeted us, and Kevin and my mother's friends found us quickly in the car park just as we arrived. Astonishingly, my mother didn't once introduce me, and I had to introduce myself after much silence and awkwardness. She never once spoke to me or referred to me the entire night. Thankfully, I was sitting next to Kevin and opposite her friend. I could fend for myself and interact pleasantly, being the natural conversationalist I am. I am always and ever interested in new people, so it wasn't a hardship to get to know them. Kevin was the life and soul of the party and treated us all to dinner. In fact, he never once let me pay for anything the entire week, which bothered my mother, and all in all we had a good night – well, except my mother, ignoring me and waiting for Kevin to have an affair, on guard the whole time.

Finally, it was time to leave Cambridgeshire and move on to visit my friend in London for a few days before travelling to Kent to join my father. We got into the car and all three of us headed to the small country train station where I would say goodbye. My heart was beating in anticipation of getting out of that hellhole! Tingling all over, we all got out of the car when we arrived at the station. I was expecting them to walk me to the platform, but my mother, standing with the car door open, said, 'Is it all right if we just drop you here? I want to get the shopping done before a delivery we are expecting at 11 a.m.'. Even Kevin looked alarmed. I felt all the air go out of my body. I looked at her and put my arms around her, at which she ever so slightly stood back. I managed to say, 'Well done on getting such a lovely new home. It's beautiful. Enjoy it'. She flinched at my words and I left it at that. I gave Kevin a big hug and thanked him for being so kind, then walked by myself to the platform with my heaving suitcase. I never looked back.

I don't think I have ever in my entire life felt so relieved to be rid of my mother. At that moment, I knew I would never speak to her again. It was time to release her from my life, as she brought only misery and pain. It took me about a month to fully decide to let her go. I didn't want to be rash and rush into a very big decision. I had thought about breaking away from her permanently for years, but she was my mother and I didn't want to hurt anyone, let alone my mother. I do genuinely and truly believe in the inherent goodness of people. It came to a point where I felt I was making this decision to cut her out of my life for me and my self-worth. I didn't want to break a relationship this important, though I saw that it was no longer good for me to be involved with her.

Weighing all the circumstances and options for truly being congruent within myself, I settled upon the decision back in Australia and decided to cut my mother completely out of my life. I now consider her lost to me, gone. I won't take a call or receive a letter or take part in any way anymore in the tangled web she weaves – not that she's tried to contact me since, nor

I her. Just because she is gone from my future doesn't mean she doesn't have a place in my past or in my heart. I feel for her, forgive her, and want her to have a better life, but not at the cost of dragging me down with her. This time, I come first, because I deserve better.

'Life is hard. Then you die. Then they throw dirt in your face. Then the worms eat you. Be grateful it happens in that order.'

David Gerrold

Chapter 8
The Beauty in Death

One of the main reasons I went back to the UK on this trip in June 2012 was because my father had increasingly been feeling unwell. He had poor health for a lot of his life, with heart attacks, strokes, and severe back pain. It had come to the point where he couldn't walk more than ten metres and needed an electric buggy to transport him around, where once he would have walked. I sensed that his time on this earth, though he was only sixty-eight, was nearly at an end. So after a brief visit to my London friend, who is in fact my brother-in-law's sister, I travelled on a fast train to Kent to meet my father, sensing it was the last time we would see each other. I was so pleased to see him, feeling relieved to be away from my mother but also anxious at seeing my father face-to-face since the incident over the phone about the molestation of my friend. As soon as I saw him and the look of pure joy to see me on his face, I felt comforted. This old, broken man had become someone that needed love in my eyes, perhaps a motherly love he hadn't received much of in his life. After heaving my heavy suitcase up a lot of steps with the help of kind strangers, I rushed over to him and threw myself into his arms, this act indicating that all was OK, that I was there and we were OK.

As my father was still very poor, I had arranged and paid for us to go on a memory lane trip – not of my memories, but of his. Before growing up in the southeast of London, he was born in picturesque Cornwall in West England. We were going on an old-fashioned road trip and we were to do nothing but sightsee and eat Cornish food. I was very excited, as I'd heard so many great things about Cornwall, though I had never been. We were to stay at his council unit in the countryside of Kent and just potter around until the trip began in a few days. Knowing my father, I knew that his place would be dirty and not pleasant to stay in, so I prepared myself to just get on with it and know we would be in Cornwall soon.

We arrived at his home, where I would sleep on the sofa as it was a one-bedroom council property. He insisted I take his bed but there was no way I was going to take it, so I won that battle and stayed on the sofa. The carpet in his house was so old and dirty that my shoes literally stuck to the soiled carpet and the place stunk of smoke and grease. What had happened to my father, who used to turn my childhood bedroom over in a rage when I hadn't cleaned it properly? I suspected that an old man living on his own for a very long time had got the better of the place.

Doing the best I could, knowing this was temporary, my father brought out my sleeping covers for my sleeping arrangements. He brought out no less than the old single bedcover and duvet I had had when I lived as a teenager in our old family home! It hadn't even been washed since then. I took it with a twisted face and he realised he should have washed it first. So, after washing and drying the covers, I was set for sleep and settled into the sofa, which was ancient and ready for bed itself. After a few hours on the sofa, it felt like there were little insects crawling around my body and I realised there may have been little animals or fleas in the furniture. I set about recreating my bed, spreading the duvet cover across the sofa, using it as a barrier between me and the old furniture and making my dressing gown my blanket. I finally went back to sleep. You may be realising that my holiday wasn't shaping up to be much of a holiday!

My mother's sister, my Aunty Chris, who had spoken to me briefly on the telephone a week before when I was at my mother's house, called me on my mobile and asked how I was surviving my parents. Having met her only once when I was five, it was weird being in touch with another family member. I was used to having a small family. She expressed knowledge that my mother was not easy to be around and that she'd like to come and meet me at my father's to take me to my grandad's, as was supposed to have happened when I had been staying at my mother's a week before. I was so thrilled and excited to be able to visit my elusive and mysterious grandfather courtesy of my Aunty. This visit was all secret squirrel business, as my mother was no longer in the picture. My father and Aunty knew each other well but hadn't seen one another for twenty-five years.

When she arrived, my dad was so pleased to see her and glad for me that someone would take me to see my grandad. I had only ever met my grandad a few times as a child. My father was appalled and yet not entirely surprised at the turn of events with my mother the week before. Sitting in my father's somewhat shambles of a house, we sipped tea and our talk turned to what I'd experienced the prior week. With eager ears the two people listened to my tale and gave me the support I needed. When recalling past times, which my and dad and I didn't do often, we recounted my being in a foster home, and I learned for the first time that he didn't know I was being fostered at the time. My aunty recoiled in horror and kept repeating the sentence 'You were fostered?' over and over again. According to her, no-one on my mother's side of the family had ever known about this. She reported that grandad would be furious about it and would never have allowed it had he known. As he was approaching his mid-eighties, I asked my aunty to keep it to herself, as it was water under the bridge. No good would come of telling him now. She promised she would, but that promise didn't last long. My father revealed that during the change from living with my foster parents to going into his care (when the nervous breakdown occurred), my mother wrote a letter to the court dealing with my custody case. He explained to me that she wrote a letter saying she thought it was best I stayed with my father as she couldn't look after me. She wouldn't be attending the court case. This in itself was new information and would have been easy enough to deal with from my perspective, save for the reality that she had accused me the very week before of choosing my father over her and said she couldn't forgive for me it!

My aunty and I soon left to visit my grandad. Very old and quite frail, he didn't leave anything to chance, asking lots of questions and seeming thrilled that I'd come to see him. He asked me why he hadn't seen much of me in life, and I was flabbergasted considering that my mother had said that no-one in her family was interested in me and that I shouldn't bother with them. I would have been so incredibly pleased to be a part of the family. As time went on, I came to realise that this was a great method of keeping people apart so she could concoct and scheme without being caught. I told grandad I would have loved to know him and that it wasn't too late, that we could be more like family now. He knew that I'd fallen out with my mother and said good riddance to her, though he never seemed to follow suit.

He secretly asked me once why the girls didn't get on, meaning his five daughters. 'How would I know?' I replied. I knew nothing of the family and was even more in the dark than he was! Getting to know this side of the family more was a treat, and I asked as many questions as I could. I didn't want to leave that day, and grandad wanted me to stay too. An unusual feeling of being wanted came over me, as I'd never felt that from my own blood on this side of the family and family systems can never be replaced or denied. It was a fulfilling feeling. Reluctantly, my aunty and I parted ways. I thanked her for going out of her way to take me to grandad and to uphold a promise that her sister, my mother, never did.

The road trip to Cornwall was fantastic. Sightseeing and gallivanting around, my father and I had a blast. There were certainly awkward moments and silences during which we didn't know what to say or how to act. I didn't want to bring up past issues – there didn't really seem to be a burning need, and I had long come to terms with them anyway. I spent another sensational week with Suzanne and her family that now consisted of Holly, who was eight, Adam, who was three, and Suzanne's husband, Colin. Seeing Suzanne's mother, Carol, and recounting my experience on this trip uncovered more information about my childhood that I didn't know about. Carol shared a couple of new bits of information with Suzanne and me. We were curious about my past, and Carol revealed that my mother would leave me at their house for long periods of time without saying when she would come back to collect me. Carol also told us that my mother was known in my early years for constant flirting with Rob, Carol's husband. Carol seemed more bemused by this particular fact than threatened. It was great to hear as an adult about my life from people who saw what was happening and made sense of it when I couldn't as a child. Being with Suzanne, Carol, and Angela was like being at home. They were my other family, one I will never forget.

Back home in Australia, the next six months went by with fantastic experiences at work. *Alive & Kicking* was growing and exceeding targets and expectations. Phil and I were happy, and he had changed jobs after ten years of service. Growing and wanting new challenges, he was working hard and expanding his own knowledge and skills, transferring them to another business that needed them.

One December evening, we were having dinner with Rosalie, the Christmas tree was glistening, and the night was growing darker and cooler after the hot Australian day. Phil and I had cleared up the dishes, Rosalie had left for her own home, and we were relaxing together. Then the dreaded call arrived. Gordon, my dad's best and oldest friend, called to advise that my father had passed away at the age of sixty-eight. I knew immediately when I heard Gordon's voice. He only called in emergency situations because he was my father's immediate next of kin in England. I knew the news was bad. With Gordon's voice in my ear, I looked across at Phil and signalled that my fears were true and my father was dead. I felt a range of emotions in that moment. I felt shocked, though not surprised. I gained a certain calm, though logistical uncertainties of the moments ahead spun through my mind – people were expecting me in England.

I was scheduled to MC a conference the very next day for my own business. I had been booked six months ago and these events are important and require all talent to turn up on the day. I was terrified – not only had my father passed of a heart attack, the gig I had to MC the next day wasn't one that was easily cancelled. I spent a few hours crying and thinking about my dad and how he never let me call in sick for anything in my life. I decided I would go ahead and facilitate hundreds of people on stage the next day. It's funny how I watch movies where people die, where the grieved are going along to the funeral, putting on their makeup, and getting on with the situation. I always say to Phil when watching those scenes that I could never do that. I would be a raving mess with no makeup and crazy clothes, not having been able to cope with the news. Well, there I was the next day; my father had passed away less than ten hours ago. I had had very little sleep and was putting on my game face, determined not to be unreliable or cause issues for my clients. I had alerted the organisers the night before of my news and asked them to help me through the day. I arrived that morning with a smile on my face, greeted them before the event was to start, and strictly instructed that no-one was to know and they weren't to mention it to me throughout the day. If there is anything I've learned in life, it is to keep going, to manage my state of mind and choose how I feel. This was no different. There would be time to grieve later – I could do this, and I did. When the event was finished, I said goodbye to the organisers, who had arranged a thank you card and a bunch of flowers for me. This is the moment I teetered and let a few tears out. I got to the car and let the tears flow, knowing that there was nothing in the way of my grief now.

Suddenly I was on the aeroplane going back to England, where I'd been just five months before, this time to arrange a funeral. Due to my father's poor financial situation, the cost was entirely on me – and Phil. No other family existed apart from the sister I had, who hadn't been in contact for years. I did manage to find her mobile number from years back when she was briefly in my dad's life. I called her and explained that our father was dead. She was empathetic for me but wouldn't be coming to the funeral. Who was I to judge? I'd cut my mother out of my life, and I'm sure there was a good reason for her to do the same with her father. I accepted that she wanted nothing more to do with him, and we never kept in contact after a few texts and general updates.

Phil and I couldn't afford for both of us to go back. Fran and Rosalie loaned us money to help with the funeral and airfare costs, these loans were paid back in the following six months. Suzanne was ready to have me at her house for a few weeks, where I shared a room with Holly, who was a gracious and wonderful young girl. Knowing nothing about how to arrange a funeral or how to close someone's accounts, clear out their house, and the like, Suzanne and I spent days working through regulations and checklists. Suzanne was a blessing once again; I could count on her without hesitation. Her family, my dad's few friends, and my own friends were unbelievably supportive. My cousin, who lived halfway across England and was probably closer to my dad than I was, did as much as she could over the phone, supporting me and talking to me. She really knew him better than anyone else did. I reconnected with Sara, my stepmother, after remembering years ago my dad had told me she worked at a pharmaceutical company.

On the off-chance she still worked there, I emailed their general information email. The email was forwarded to Sara because she was now working at a different company. The employee who received my email was still in contact with her and thankfully sent it on. I thought it only right that she be notified. She and my father didn't end their relationship on bad terms. It was nerve-wracking meeting her before the funeral and catching up on the years that had passed. I had seen her last when I was fifteen, and now here I was thirty-three and grown up. Sara is a kind and wonderful person, who I will be in touch with for as long as I can foresee. I do believe that despite the circumstances of her age when she met my father, she was the love of his life.

Admittedly, I didn't have a terrible time at my father's funeral. I was determined to make it as fun and controversial as he was. He loved tea and always said that when he was dead he'd haunt me with tea bags, as I must have made thousands of cups of tea when I was young. So we made tea bag wreaths. No flowers, just his motorbike helmet and a photo of us on one of his trips to Australia. At the end of the humorous and moving service, I played his favourite song of all time, Black Sabbath's 'Paranoid'. If you haven't heard it, just Google it. It's a crazy heavy metal song and not a song I suspect had ever been played full blast in this funeral home until my father's funeral. People from the past who I hadn't seen for a very long time were there. Suzanne and Sara were like my guardians, supporting me and keeping me close. Gordon, Dad's friend, was brilliant, especially considering he was close to eighty. He helped me both emotionally and physically, along with a few other friends of Dad's who I didn't know very well. They came to clear his house and sell what we could to recoup the cost of the funeral.

During this entire event, all I saw was kindness, beauty, and togetherness. I smiled through the whole experience, grateful for the opportunity to connect with my past in such a sensational way. We celebrated the life of the troubled man who was my father and gave thanks to those who supported him and me. For it is our choice, isn't it, how we react to and experience life? We can mourn and cry, feel pain and loss, or we can all choose to feel and see the good people bring when they are together, united. This experience just made me more determined to use every ounce of my being to live to the fullest, explore, help, support, and grow in all forms with all people. Never will I waste a single drop of my existence on anything that doesn't help me expand and love. I allowed my grief to happen; I didn't limit it or ask it to leave. I experienced it fully, and when it had taken its path I let it go and held only the knowledge that the very last words my father and I said to each other the very day before he died were 'I love you my darling' and 'I love you too, Dad'.

Spending time with Suzanne and her family for those few weeks really gave me time to be away from all the stress and be connected with a family unit. Reflecting a lot whilst I was there, it dawned on me that I had now officially lost both of my parents. Of course, I lost one to death and another to a different kind of loss. I was starting to feel mixtures of feelings. Part of me mourned the fact that I was now parentless whilst the other, more prominent part of me felt relief. I was no longer chained to either of them and it felt shamefully good. When I think of feeling shame, it occurs to me that it's natural to feel bad about being relieved from the departure of loved ones – either through death or when gone in another way – and after pondering these feelings and thoughts for a few weeks I quickly respected my own emotions and allowed myself to have them, to feel how I did without judgement. I concluded that I should be relieved after all this time, looking back on my life and all the experiences I'd had, and knew that it's only me that allows the feeling of shame based on society's expectations of how I 'should' feel. So I decided to feel free and to be grateful for all the experiences I had with both of the people called my parents and move on.

Because I was back in England, I had another opportunity to see my grandad, so I made time to drive to his home and visit one more time. We had brilliant talks about love, life, and his own long life. My grandad was always watching Australian border security programs and questioned me constantly about what you can and can't bring into the country! My mother didn't know until after I left to go back to Australia that I'd been in England that December and that my father had passed away. Apparently, according to my aunty, my grandad let it slip a few weeks later.

Before I left to get on the plane for my second trip back to Australia that year, Suzanne's family invited me to a Christmas dinner. Angela wouldn't be there for Christmas due to going away to the US with her family for a holiday, so they held a special extra Christmas Day the week before the real one. To be included once again, just like when I was a child, with no-one to stop me or tell me I couldn't, and to truly enjoy the feeling of family with them once more was an astonishing experience. The minute I entered the house with all the blaring Christmas lights, the music, and the smell of turkey, I was greeted with a warm, excited cuddle from Carol and promptly told to put on a pair of elf slippers before scurrying in to see the rest of the family. It was hard for me to hold back my emotions that day, as it represented everything I'd ever cherished about my surrogate family. I still suspect they don't really know what it means to me. After dinner, in the warm room with the cold below-freezing temperature outside, I fell asleep on the sofa between Colin and a great big teddy bear. I was secure in myself after what had been a long and stressful year. I acted just as you should with family at Christmas.

'When something goes wrong in your life, just yell 'Plot twist!' and move on.'

Author Unknown

Chapter 9
One Life Stand

The concept of flourishing came into my life quite by surprise. Once it entered it was abundant and relentless in its pursuit of me – well, as much as a word or concept can be relentless. I distinctly recall the very moment the word 'flourish' hit my soul. It was much akin to water hitting the ground in a downpour: impactful and unmistakable. I was sitting in a boardroom in the middle of Perth city. Jacqui, an acquaintance of mine, was presenting to a group of executives at a breakfast I was hosting. She was providing the group with much food for thought and was trying to get practical feedback on her PhD research. Her research covered some breathtaking, and I mean breathtaking work that looked at ethics in leadership. I was taken aback by her questions and riveted by her findings when she presented the word 'eudemonia'. Upon speaking this word and seeing the baffled expressions on the faces in the audience, she broke the meaning down to its very core to explain the concept that sits under the word: human flourishing. Aristotle, she explained, had produced works that talk about the virtues of human beings. He correlated ethics and virtues to how humans flourish, how they ultimately embark upon finding and experience happiness. Through all my studies and exposure to this point, I'd never heard these words, and their meaning resonated with me deeply.

Once I'd connected with this word 'flourish', it appeared everywhere! People were describing me as someone who had flourished. Customers told me that they saw my business flourishing. Each time the word surfaced, it stopped me in my tracks. I began to relate more and more to the fact that I inherently believe in human flourishing. In fact, the very core of who I am wants each person in this world to feel at some point and for as long as possible what it is like to flourish – to feel the effects of the impact of flourishing. I certainly have. This book is not about my story for the sake of telling a story. This book is about the strength, perseverance, and the sheer desire of wanting to live and live with all my might, and more importantly 'how' to live, even with the hard times that occurred. People meet me and often think I had a private education, that I met my husband at school as a high school sweetheart and that I come from a family of money. It's funny, isn't it? Why? Because their judgement is a projection of what they want to see. Perhaps they want to believe people exist in this perfect world. Often their beliefs reinforce that they will never have that, and that therefore they shouldn't even try for more than what they have (physically or emotionally). I understand why this happens, though it shows me that these individuals have lost hope within their perception. They are often hanging onto untrue stories that will not serve them. How do I respond to these misguided perceptions, you may wonder? I seek to express that I too am human; I too have doubts, uncertainties, difficult days, and sad moments in my life. People are not perfect. Life is not perfect. I believe it is how we deal with what comes our way that is the skill to hone. I revel in explaining my story to people as they often experience – even unconsciously right in front of me – for one moment that it *is* possible that they can have the life they dream of. That's all I ask for – a possibility. If the brain can conceive something, it can be achieved. If my story supports a person in shifting their view, then they open to all that can be.

Understanding how we construct our own reality and experiences is empowering. Once we understand this we can shape what we want to have happen in our life, what we want to feel, see, think. I often think of conflict as moving between old beliefs and truths into new unchartered beliefs and a new reality. The moving between the parts can cause confusion and unrest. Being aware of this occurrence and stepping outside of ourselves, seeing ourselves whilst looking from above, is a skill in itself. The ability to be flexible, to disconnect and reconnect, rather than the sense of feeling controlled by our environment – I believe that's the skill that's important.

Often when working with my clients I ask the person to assess what's real. 'Tell me the facts', I say, 'Separate the emotion'. Where is your evidence? What's real? When people ask this of themselves they soon realise that the emotion or story that is grabbing hold of them and taking them off track is a deluded (albeit well intentioned) mindset habit. These patterns of thinking often occur from way back in the past and, perhaps, from believing something that used to be true and is no longer true. My role as a coach is to support the person in taking what no longer serves them and turning their belief or habit into something new that will support their reason for being on this earth. Am I different from you? Yes and no. Yes because we are all unique; no because we have the same ability to construct our own reality, to choose the ways we deal with hardship through to excitement. I'm no more special than you. I've decided to take what I've experienced in all facets and hone it to produce an outstanding, positive contribution to the world in which I live. When I'm coaching with a client I can emphatically say that I am being the best version of myself I can possibly be. Being with a client one on one and working at the deepest level possible cannot be replaced by anything. I have found what it takes for Suzanne – me – to flourish. Building my own business whilst studying for my master's degree in coaching, writing this book, and working with *Alive & Kicking* for four days a week has taught me that when we are on a path, a path that is absolutely congruent with our core values and aligns with a life purpose, results can and will happen. Believe me: during the busy time since starting this book, a lot has happened even today to confront me.

My grandad passed away, Phil and I moved house and sold a house, and my beautiful cat Bobby – who I'd had for fourteen years – passed away. All of this happened whilst I was dealing with an ongoing court case. With these events transpiring within a span of three months, I can tell you I had some seriously stroppy, difficult, and questioning days. There were times when I didn't recognise my own thoughts. People look at me and wonder how I cope, how it is I bounce back so quickly. I believe it is how we deal with these situations whilst staying true to who we are that is the important skill. It's being able to be gentle with ourselves, to allow ourselves the courtesy to feel without judgement. I believe that putting a time limit on negative emotions and transforming our choices back onto our path with acceptance and forgiveness is a way of moving into a place of abundance and certainty and hope. There is always polarity in life: light and dark, night and day, happy and sad. Nothing exists without its opposite, otherwise we wouldn't have the ability to compare or experience.

If the last thirty-five years are anything to compare to, the next sixty will be incredible. Spending so many years in turmoil, escaping and running, changing directions at the drop of a hat, protecting and defending myself, I can honestly reveal that I wouldn't change a single thing; all that has transpired contributes to who I am today. I am truly thankful for every single experience and now know exactly what I stand for.

I stand for kindness, both the giving of it and the ability to receive, for without the kindness of strangers, how would I ever have learned to see beyond myself like they did? I stand for being kind in the smallest of ways and never knowing the impact of that action, doing or being something that signifies and expresses who you are and how you contribute to the greater world as well as your own. As Wilbert taught me over the past few years, we are connected through an energetic field through which when we are aware and open, without restriction or too much ego, but with soul and positive intention, we can and will create anything.

I stand for self-belief. To trust oneself comes first, to believe that you are possible and that what you set your sights on is possible with effort and time. Fran showed me that all can be achieved; the question is not 'what?' or 'why?' once you know what you want, only 'how?' If someone else has achieved what you or I want to achieve, then how are we any different to him or her? One human is not born with any extra special skill – everything can be replicated and learned. None of us were born being able to cook, coach, lead, or write a book; we had to learn. We can also learn how to think, feel, and act. For most of my life, I've been true to myself, and when I realised I wasn't, I owned my behaviour and my mistakes and continued to build what is important within myself. Whilst it's only in the past few years that I've been able to take those inner strategies and put names, frameworks, labels, and identities to them, I've known within myself that trusting and believing in myself is essential. When we don't believe or trust ourselves, we stumble, hold back, fight, defend, and let old baggage and old stories get in the way.

I stand for choice. People very often do not realise that we each have choice in every circumstance. It is very easy to think that there is no choice. I've heard people express: 'I simply had to come to work today; I had no choice' or 'I had to tell him that lie; I had no choice' or 'She made me feel that way; I had no choice in the matter'. Understanding that we each have our own choices and that with every choice comes consequences, good or bad, is essential to taking responsibility and being empowered. I could choose not to go to work, and then I wouldn't have money for my mortgage. It's still a choice. This is where 'learning to learn' comes in, as the more education and exposure we get access to, the more likely it is that we will learn how to build, create, and expand what we want and who we are in life. I believe that belief in the self comes first, as it is only when we think we can do something that we will find a way. There are plenty of rules we set up in our mind and body that become habits and then settle in. In my view, the key to life is flexibility – The Law of Requisite Variety – because if we as humans don't shift, morph, grow, and flex, then we stay still, stable, and stagnant. Curiosity didn't kill the cat, it expanded him! Increasing self-trust and growing our competence in any given area increases self-belief. There are always ways to get or be how we want.

I believe in my One Life Stand: my husband Phil. How is it that a girl who once slept around and couldn't stick or commit to much has lived her life with a man who has given her the greatest gifts any human could give another? Phil has given me hope and showed me what it is to persevere and work for what you want. He has shown me how to be kind, to learn, to believe, and to achieve; he has shown me what it is to love and be loved unconditionally. He said to me many years ago that I was destined for great things. Only now have I begun to believe him.

Many people ask me how it is we managed not only to stay together all these years, but more importantly how it is that every single year gets better and better in our relationship. I tell them this: we are thoroughly honest; we do not hide a single thought or feeling. We trust that even in the hardest of moments and the darkest of times we have each other's back and will be generous in our understanding and spirit. Phil and I are completely different. I am vivacious, gregarious, crazy, and love risk and change. I'm talkative, optimistic, and love being the centre of attention. Phil is quieter, supportive, logical, thorough, detailed, consistent, persistent, practical, and sometimes a little more cynical than me. We enjoy different activities and have learned to build each other's strengths and see our differences as something that makes us strong as a unit, complementary. We stand next to each other side-by-side. We take turns to shoulder the burden and take care of each other. We are kindred spirits because we worked hard to be. He is my One Life Stand.

My mother-in-law, or as I call her, MIL, Rosalie, was right. It's printed now, Rosalie! I could have done with emulating Phil years ago. It was the hardest and best advice she ever gave me. Over the years, with more understanding on her part and compassion and respect on mine, we have become closer than I ever was with my own mother. In fact, many people think we are mother and daughter, which is hilarious, as we look absolutely nothing alike. It's in the way we act, and we don't correct them anymore. I am blessed to have such a supportive in-law family, in which my sister-in-law has graced the family with a son, George, who is the centre of attention and a joy to watch, grow, and expand in his own way. Anne and Richard are marvellous parents; it's their destiny.

My friends have become a major resting post for me as I have learned to let them in and open up my vulnerabilities. I do like to think I'm right and that I am a 'know it all' sometimes, so I like having friends who level me, argue with me, and talk straight. I don't have time to dillydally, skirting around what's real. Relationships are essential to me; they are what make my world go round, connecting with people and sharing emotion with the highs and the lows. I have made a conscious decision to only associate with people who are willing to give as much in the relationship as I do. I totally understand that there are swings and roundabouts, and for friendship I will give everything and expect the same in return.

In October 2012 I created something very meaningful and surprising: a business. Studying for my master's in applied coaching, I knew I had found my calling. Before coaching I didn't even believe in a calling, and I now know that within myself my calling, my destiny, is to assist others in intimately exploring their innermost lightest and darkest thoughts. This is crucial to discovering and knowing yourself. So I set up a business that supports people to have a life worth living. I attract people from all different walks of life, ranging from seventeen-year-olds who don't know what to do with their lives to general managers who want to lead their teams more effectively to CEOs who are having issues with trust in their business to entrepreneurs who want to create and impact the world with something big but feel stuck to people of all types who feel lost and confused. It seems there is little that I haven't heard in all these different humans, and every single person inspires me. I learn from my clients as much as they get from our interaction.

It's amazing to think that after all this time and all that I have experienced, I now get the opportunity to help others around the world fulfil their lives and dreams. It is a privilege. Sure, I will grow more and learn more and have hard times, though it seems to me that I have experienced enough to be able to cope with most situations. I just think that my frame of view has stretched so far that most problems in other people's eyes don't seem like problems to me, just another experience to be worked out. My purpose and dream is to support people to live life on purpose. So many people correct me with this, saying it should read 'live life with purpose'. 'No, it's not' I reply! It is correct. Live life 'on' purpose. Dream, create, build, explore. I want for people the very best being alive has to offer, no matter what. Human potential and personal growth is something everyone has access to, and the people who shift their thinking and start to see beyond just themselves, the people who realise they can control their environment and emotions, who know it will take work, commitment, and perseverance, and that yes, they will need to trust and believe in themselves and fall down and stand up again. 'It's OK', I say, 'I will support you, as I already believe in you.' The question is: are you ready? For who are you *not* to flourish?

Acknowledgments

This is the part of the book where words seem to be the hardest to find. Not because there is little feeling, genuinely because there are so very many feelings. How can my gratitude possibly be restricted to the written word when my heart is very much involved?

To acknowledge someone is to express gratitude, to show that you have heard or seen or experienced with them. There are many people I would like to acknowledge.

First, it's important to mention all the people who have been mentioned in this book. Without your part to play in my life, this book wouldn't exist. Thank you for supporting me, guiding me, and being with me in my adventure so far.

Thank you Tony Inman; you introduced me to the lovely Emily Gowor – my book mentor, publisher, and crazy new friend. Emily you have been absolutely pivotal in the creation and realisation of this book. Your feedback and patience in writing "this sentence is confusing" hundreds of times is admirable! You have an amazing future ahead of you and I believe you will achieve more and more great things. My editor

Ashton for creating approximately 6000 changes to my book and for showing how grammar really should be expressed! Joanna Bryant, for agreeing to proofread and put her amazing wordsmith detailed ability to the test. For her honesty in telling me some difficult feedback too - I honour her input and friendship.

To Rhi, my project manager, thank you for coming in so strong at the end. To the typesetter and the official proofreader who got the book finished, your attention to detail is also incredible! Wow, there are so many people involved in creating a story to come to life.

Fran Berry, you are an exquisite person. You have shown me what it is to 'create' a life. Phil and I are eternally grateful that you have graced us with your presence. You are a true and beautiful friend.

It cannot go without saying that Picco's Kitchen (Poach Pear) has been an essential part of my book writing. Whilst waiting for my coffee (one of many), the book title came to me. I distinctly remember the team there were running around finding me sticky notes and pens to record my ideas! They all gathered around my table and we agreed that *A Flourishing Mind* was a great title! They kept me going with yummy food, coffee, and love.

Jacqui Boaks, you inspired me greatly when you spoke on those mornings in Perth. You helped me to find human flourishing. Even though you say Aristotle is who I should be thanking, I thank you for bringing him to me.

I have to thank my gorgeous, unconditionally loving friends, who manage to keep smiling even when I've got another crazy idea, like writing a book! Your support and encouragement never ceases to fuel me. You've taught me to love fully and give all of myself to you in friendship. Thank you Sarah M., Melinda, Beth, Kelly, Jeremy, Cheryl Honeymama, Jeff, Lou, Rod and Jaymelee.

A special mention to Melinda, who was the muse for this book cover – Mel, I know the tree isn't quite what you had in mind, and if it weren't for you, the tree wouldn't have been 'born'. I love it!

I learn from my clients every single day. Thanks to them for being amazing humans who actively take part in their own lives. To see the changes you all make and with such gusto is inspiring.

Wilbert Molenaar, you have taught me so very much. Yes, you were my NLP teacher, and you have also taught me about my life. You don't let me hide or abdicate. What you have to teach may sometimes be confronting, but my goodness it's been priceless to me. You are extraordinary. Thank you.

My cousin Lisa – my only family left. In some ways I want to shout 'We made it!' Thanks for being such a great supporter on the other side of the world. Although we don't see each other much now, I am so grateful for your presence and I cherish our relationship.

My beautiful cat, Bobby. You always slept by my side, keeping your energy close and full of love (whilst biting Phil). Thanks for treading all over my keyboard and messing up my book on occasion. Being a close part of my life for fourteen years, more than most other living people is remarkable and I miss you every single day.

To you, the reader. As you've made it this far, I thank you for reading and taking the time for yourself to experience through my eyes. It's always daunting writing a book, hoping that the reader will get something from it that is valuable in their own life. I hope you have experienced a valuable insight or 'aha' moment along the way.

To the people who are the dearest to my heart: Robyn, Suzanne, and Rosalie. You are incredibly important to me and you have shown me such compassion, kindness, and love. Without you, this book would not have been possible. Without you, my beliefs in myself would be weaker. You have been the family I needed.

My darling husband Phil. 'Above all else, no matter what, we have each other.' So many times in our lives we have repeated those words. In all the adversity, hurdles and beauty that has occurred in either of our lives, we repeat those words and it all seems that little bit easier. I think of you every moment of every day. You are my world. Thank you for being you and for supporting me to find who I am. I will always be yours.

A Flourishing Mind

Working with Suzanne

Personal and Professional Coaching – names are anonymous due to the sensitive nature of one on one coaching. I am often advised to put full names for marketing reasons, however I just won't break confidentiality!

"As a leader of leaders I have had the pleasure of hiring Suzanne as both a Coach and Facilitator for my teams on more than one occasion over the past four years. In all engagements her professionalism, enthusiasm, ability to connect with people and absolute passion for her craft has been extraordinary. There are not many people who truly put their heart and soul into everything they do, but Suzanne is one of the rare few."

G.Y. – Group Manager

"As we went through the coaching journey, I learned so much about myself and the strength I have within me. It has taught me that there is so much within me and by developing my strengths and identifying my weaknesses, I can be better in every aspect of my life; personal and working. I would urge anyone to take this journey, it's really one of self-discovery; and its amazing what you can actually learn about yourself! We are complex creatures! Thanks again to my great coach for my new-found strength and confidence. I promise to keep checking in with myself and to continue to ride the beautiful wave that I am now on.'

Assessment Manager

"Working with Suzanne was the best decision I have made in my adult life! Even though I was not clear on 'what' needed to change – I know I was fed up with repeating the same patterns that were making up my life. Each session was challenging & taught me to grow in ways I did not know were possible. Personal growth can be painful – but I was so beautifully held and supported by Suzanne each & every time. I would recommend her to anyone who wants more out of life – even if you don't know what that more is – Suzanne will coax it out of you & help you shine in so many ways."

M.A. – Finance Coordinator

"In particular the one on one coaching provided the most significant benefit to me personally and professionally as a leader. The coaching sessions took me through a journey from uncertainty and what felt like a lack of control in my working life to an understanding of what makes me tick and motivates me to achieve, and now a sense of empowerment. Really, all of the information and control was in my head, my coach just provided me with a way to get it out and understand it."

T.A. – Customer Service Manager

"With your kind and gentle non-judgemental approach you steered me to finding a better version of me...one better equipped to deal with the stresses and pain in my life. What I learned from your coaching not only enabled me to get through a very difficult time (and continues to) but has also equipped me with tools and a new outlook that I am 100% certain I will use for the rest of my life...you are a treasure! In a world that can foster selfishness and negativity you have shown the beauty of a giving and selfless soul and I am forever in your debt."

S.M. – Teacher

"In just three hours Suzanne really helped me to understand what makes me 'tick' and equip me to handle those situations that trigger an emotional response in the workplace. I have seen an enormous change in my ability to cope with those triggered events and also have been working hard to validate myself rather than seek validation from others. She was compassionate and I felt she really cared about me as a person – yet still maintained her professionalism. She really set the standard when it comes to coaching and if I could get even marginally close to her ability I would be a much better leader and coach."

R.S. – Executive Strategy Manager

"I had the pleasure of having Suzanne as a mentor/ coach earlier this year (2014). I found our meetings to be very helpful in getting my start-up off the ground. After our meetings I would feel fully energised and focused on taking the next step in business. Suzanne's positive & focused outlook helped me to keep on track. The pitching techniques I learned were very useful. Suzanne introduced me to other business owners who had also been through the same procedures, all of whom help me greatly."

P.H. – Entrepreneur

"I recently had the honor of meeting Suzanne at the Perth Global Women's Summit and was instantly taken with her bright and sunny outlook on life. Little did I know, the depth of knowledge this dynamo held until she kindly offered a few tips on how to make my presentations even better! One forty-five minute Skype session with her and I was armed with some of the most powerful tools and tips I have ever known. I highly recommend Suzanne as a powerful, professional and genuine people person."

B.C. – Cultural Facilitator

Speaking, MC & Facilitation

"Suzanne recently hosted an evening function to launch our new premises. What an inspired choice for an MC! She managed the event seamlessly, bringing her own unique style of humour, professionalism and engagement with our clients and business partners. With her bubbly personality, Suzanne has the capacity to take control of activities and balance important business messages with just the right amount of light-hearted humour. She has an enviable talent for knowing just what to say and just when to say it!"

Joy Northover Director – Staff Link Group

"Suzanne is an absolute dynamo whether it be one on one, in the classroom or fronting a large conference group. Her energy is infectious and her ability to engage and challenge means she always draws the most from participants."

Libby Atkins Manager – Dept. of Housing

"Suzanne is a wonderfully engaging, dynamic, entertaining and motivating facilitator, presenter and speaker. It's impossible not to be lifted and inspired by her!"

Jo Pownall – Human Capital Consulting

"I have seen Suzanne in action over the past five years and would highly recommend her as a coach, speaker and master of ceremonies. Suzanne is engaging, funny, articulate, interesting, lively and entertaining. Suzanne lights up a room."

Elizabeth Thair – Career Pathways

"I asked Suzanne to facilitate some meetings for a group of senior leaders who were all coming together to form a new partnership. The group had representatives from eight different organisation's, with 8 different agendas. Suzanne did a great job of facilitating these discussions through the storming/norming/forming stage, and always maintained a strong focus on the outcomes and objectives, while also ensuring that a level of positive energy and collaboration was achieved. Suzanne has strong active listening and questioning skills, as well as an effectively disarming manner!"

Craig Spencer – Head of Community, Bankwest

Visit www.suzannewaldron.com for more inspiring articles, videos and community interaction to support your life worth living.

About The Author

When supporting others to create more freedom, clarity, drive and success in their lives, Suzanne Waldron is at her happiest. In fact she describes being with others in this capacity as being the best version of herself. She supports others to have a life worth living.

Whilst Suzanne knows her human behavioural change qualifications are important, it's the life lessons she's learned along the way that really qualifies her. Having had a difficult life for many of her earlier years such as living with a foster family, leaving home at 15 years old, being homeless and having many difficult experiences through her teens and twenties – it's these experiences and lessons that inspired Suzanne to find the peace, happiness and success that she enjoys today.

She truly believes anything is possible. Learning to believe in yourself, understand you always have a choice and acting with kindness are the key ingredients to propel you towards anything you desire. 'These three areas of self development enable a shift, a platform in which when mastered, everything else is possible.'

Originally from the UK, Suzanne is now living in Western Australia with her husband of eighteen years. She relishes in exploring cultures around the world, learning about and creating new and exciting opportunities in her business. Writing, coaching and speaking, she travels and reaches more people with her messages than ever before.

Suzanne's qualifications:

- Internationally Accredited ICF Coach
- Certified Supervisor Coaching and NLP
- Internationally Accredited Master NLP Practitioner (Neuro-Linguistic Programming)
- Masters Degree in Applied Coaching
- Advanced Diploma's in Management and Customer Contact.

Suzanne contributes to society in many ways. She is a volunteer Board Director for Uniting for Homeless and she regularly donates her coaching services to people in difficult situations. For her Masters Degree in Coaching Suzanne researched people who work in the prosocial space, so as to model their attitudes and strategies with the aim to develop more prosocial people doing more community and positive leadership activities around the world.

www.ingramcontent.com/pod-product-compliance
Ingram Content Group UK Ltd.
Pitfield, Milton Keynes, MK11 3LW, UK
UKHW041301180426
11947UKWH00009B/603